Focus in Grade 5
Teaching with Curriculum Focal Points

Focus in Grade 5

Teaching with Curriculum Focal Points

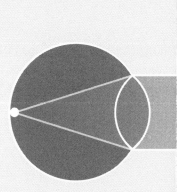

WITH BEST WISHES

Karen C Fuson

HOUGHTON MIFFLIN HARCOURT

Sybilla Beckmann, *Editor*
University of Georgia

Planning and Writing Team

Karen C. Fuson, *Northwestern University, Professor Emerita*
John SanGiovanni, *Howard County Public Schools, Maryland*
Thomasenia Lott Adams, *University of Florida*

NCTM
NATIONAL COUNCIL OF
TEACHERS OF MATHEMATICS

Copyright © 2009 by
THE NATIONAL COUNCIL OF TEACHERS OF MATHEMATICS, INC.
1906 Association Drive, Reston, VA 20191-1502
(703) 620-9840; (800) 235-7566; www.nctm.org
All rights reserved

Library of Congress Cataloging-in-Publication Data

Focus in grade 5 / Sybilla Beckmann, editor ; planning and writing team, Karen C. Fuson,
John SanGiovanni, Thomasenia Lott Adams.
    p. cm. — (Teaching with curriculum focal points)
  Includes bibliographical references.
  ISBN 978-0-87353-614-1 (alk. paper)
  1. Mathematics—Study and teaching (Elementary) —United States—Standards. 2. Fifth grade
(Education) —Curricula—United States—Standards. 3. Curriculum planning—United States. I.
Beckmann, Sybilla. II. Fuson, Karen C. III. SanGiovanni, John. IV. Adams, Thomasenia Lott. V. Title:
Focus in grade five.
  QA135.6.F63 2009
  372.7—dc22
                                                        2009005064

The National Council of Teachers of Mathematics is a public voice of mathematics education, providing
vision, leadership, and professional development to support teachers in ensuring equitable mathematics
learning of the highest quality for all students.

Printed in the United States of America

Contents

Contents

Contents

Contents

On September 12, 2006, the National Council of Teachers of Mathematics released *Curriculum Focal Points for Prekindergarten through Grade 8 Mathematics: A Quest for Coherence* to encourage discussions at the national, state, and district levels on the importance of designing a coherent elementary school mathematics curriculum focusing on the important mathematical ideas at each grade level. The natural question that followed the release of *Curriculum Focal Points* was "How do we translate this view of a focused curriculum into the classroom?"

Focus in Grade 5, one in a series of grade-level publications, is designed to support teachers, supervisors, and coordinators as they begin the discussion of a more focused curriculum across and within prekindergarten through eighth grade, as presented in *Curriculum Focal Points.* Additionally, teacher educators should find it useful as a vehicle for exploring mathematical ideas and curriculum issues involving the grade 5 mathematics curriculum with their preservice teachers.

The members of the planning and writing team, all active leaders in mathematics education and professional development, created this grade-level book as a framework for lesson-study-type experiences in which teachers deepen their understanding of the mathematical ideas they will be teaching. This book describes and illustrates instructional progressions for the mathematical concepts and skills of each fifth-grade Focal Point, including problems for students and powerful representational supports for teaching and learning that can facilitate understanding, stimulate productive discussions about mathematical thinking, and provide a foundation for fluency with the core ideas. We also discuss common student errors and misconceptions, reasons the errors may arise, and teaching methods or visual representations to address the errors. Because instructional progressions cut across grades, we have included some discussion of related Focal Points at grades 3 and 4 so that we can describe and clarify prerequisite knowledge and show how the grade 5 understandings build on what went before. To a lesser extent, we describe how the instructional progressions progress to grade 6 and beyond.

Whether you are working with your colleagues or individually, we hope you will find the discussions of the learning paths, representations, problems, and lines of reasoning valuable as you plan activities and discussions for your students and as you strive to help your students achieve the depth of understanding of important mathematical concepts necessary for their future success.

—Sybilla Beckmann, for the
Grade 5 Planning and Writing Team

As states and local school districts implement more rigorous assessment and accountability systems, teachers often face long lists of mathematics topics or learning expectations to address at each grade level, with many topics repeating from year to year. Lacking clear, consistent priorities and focus, teachers stretch to find the time to present important mathematical topics effectively and in depth.

The National Council of Teachers of Mathematics (NCTM) is responding to this challenge by presenting *Curriculum Focal Points for Prekindergarten through Grade 8 Mathematics: A Quest for Coherence. Building on Principles and Standards for School Mathematics* (NCTM 2000), this new publication is offered as a starting point in a dialogue on what is important at particular levels of instruction and as an initial step toward a more coherent, focused curriculum in this country.

The writing team for *Curriculum Focal Points for Prekindergarten through Grade 8 Mathematics* consisted of nine members, with at least one university-level mathematics educator or mathematician and one pre-K–8 classroom practitioner from each of the three grade bands (pre-K–grade 2, grades 3–5, and grades 6–8). The writing team examined curricula from multiple states and countries as well as a wide array of researchers' and experts' writings in creating a set of focal points for pre-K–grade 8 mathematics.

On behalf of the Board of Directors, we thank everyone who helped make this publication possible.

Cathy Seeley
President, 2004–2006
National Council of Teachers of Mathematics

Francis (Skip) Fennell
President, 2006–2008
National Council of Teachers of Mathematics

Members of the Curriculum Focal Points for Grades PK–8 Writing Team

Jane F. Schielack, *Chair,* Texas A&M University, College Station, Texas
Sybilla Beckmann, University of Georgia, Athens, Georgia
Randall I. Charles, San José State University (emeritus), San José, California
Douglas H. Clements, University at Buffalo, State University of New York, Buffalo, New York
Paula B. Duckett, District of Columbia Public Schools (retired), Washington, D.C.
Francis (Skip) Fennell, McDaniel College, Westminster, Maryland
Sharon L. Lewandowski, Bryant Woods Elementary School, Columbia, Maryland
Emma Treviño, Charles A. Dana Center, University of Texas at Austin, Austin, Texas
Rose Mary Zbiek, The Pennsylvania State University, University Park, Pennsylvania

Staff Liaison
Melanie S. Ott, National Council of Teachers of Mathematics, Reston, Virginia

ACKNOWLEDGMENTS

The National Council of Teachers of Mathematics would like to thank Richard Askey, Catherine Fosnot, Henry S. Kepner, Jr., and Connie Laughlin for helpful comments on drafts of the manuscript. Special thanks are due to Francis (Skip) Fennell for initiating the project and for his enthusiastic support and encouragement.

Curriculum Focal Points Grade 5 Development Team

Sybilla Beckmann, Chair
University of Georgia

Karen C. Fuson
Northwestern University

John SanGiovanni
Howard County (Maryland) Public Schools

Thomasenia L. Adams
University of Florida

Thanks also are extended to the Curriculum Focal Points Grade-band 3–5 Development Team:

Jane F. Schielack, Chair
Texas A & M University

Bonnie Ennis
Wicomico County (Maryland) Board of Education

Susan Friel
University of North Carolina

Steve Klass
San Diego State University

Purpose of This Guide

Your first question when looking at NCTM's Curriculum Focal Points might be, *How can I use NCTM's Focal Points with the local and state curriculum I am expected to teach?* The intent of this guide is to help instructional leaders and classroom teachers build focus into the curriculum that they are expected to teach through connecting related ideas and prioritizing topics of emphasis at each grade level. NCTM's Curriculum Focal Points documents are not intended to be a national curriculum but have been developed to help bring more consistency to mathematics curricula across the country. Collectively, they constitute a framework of how curricula might be organized at each grade level, prekindergarten through grade 8. They are also intended to help bring about discussion within and across states and school districts about the important mathematical ideas to be taught at each grade level. Because of the current variation among states' curricula, the Curriculum Focal Points are not likely to match up perfectly with any state curriculum. This volume, a guide to the Focal Points for grade 5, explores the mathematics that is emphasized in a focused curriculum,. Additional grade-level and grade band books will be developed by NCTM to help teachers translate the focal points identified for their grade level into coherent and meaningful instruction. Taken together, this grade 5 guide and the grade 3–5 grade-band guide can be used for teachers' professional development experiences as well as by individual classroom teachers.

Purpose of Curriculum Focal Points

The mathematics curriculum in the United States has often been characterized as a "mile wide and an inch deep." Many topics are studied each year—often reviewing much that was covered in previous years—and little depth is added each time the topic is addressed. In contrast, higher performing countries tend to select a few fundamental topics each year and develop them in greater depth. In addition, because education has always been locally controlled in the United States, learning expectations can significantly differ by state and local school systems.

In the 1980s, the National Council of Teachers of Mathematics (NCTM) began the process of bringing about change to school mathematics programs, particularly with the first document to outline standards in mathematics, titled *Curriculum and Evaluation Standards for School Mathematics* (NCTM 1989). This document provided major direction to states and school districts in developing their curricula. NCTM's *Principles and Standards for School Mathematics* (2000) further elaborated on the ideas of the 1989 Standards, outlining learning expectations in the grade bands of pre-K–2, 3–5, 6–8, and 9–12. *Principles and Standards* also highlighted six principles,

A curriculum is more than a collection of activities: It must be coherent, focused on important mathematics, and well articulated across the grades.

—The Curriculum Principle,
Principles and Standards for School Mathematics

The intent of this guide is to help instructional leaders and classroom teachers build focus into the curriculum that they are expected to teach through connecting related ideas and prioritizing topics of emphasis at each grade level.

which included the Curriculum Principle, to offer guidance for developing mathematics programs. The Curriculum Principle emphasized the need to link with, and build on, mathematical ideas as students progress through the grades, deepening their mathematical knowledge over time.

NCTM's *Curriculum Focal Points for Prekindergarten through Grade 8 Mathematics: A Quest for Coherence* (2006) is the next step in helping states and local districts refocus their curriculum. It provides an example of a focused and coherent curriculum in prekindergarten through grade 8 by identifying the most important mathematical topics or "focal points" at each grade level. The focal points are not discrete topics to be taught and checked off, but rather a cluster of related knowledge, skills, and concepts. By organizing and prioritizing curriculum and instruction in grades pre-K–8 around focus points at each grade level, teachers can foster more-cumulative learning of mathematics by students, and students' work in the later grades will build on and deepen what they learned in the earlier grades. Organizing mathematics content in this way will help ensure a solid mathematical foundation for high school mathematics and beyond.

> It provides an example of a focused and coherent curriculum in prekindergarten through grade 8 by identifying the most important mathematical topics or "focal points" at each grade level.

Impact of Focal Points on Curriculum, Instruction, and Assessment

Significant improvement can be made in the areas of curriculum, instruction, and assessment by identifying focal points at each grade level. At the curriculum level, focal points will allow for more-rigorous and in-depth study of important mathematics at each grade level. This rigor will translate to a more meaningful curriculum that students can understand and apply, thereby ensuring student learning and an increase in student achievement. At the instructional level, focal points will allow teachers to more fully know the core topics they are responsible for teaching. Teachers will not be necessarily teaching *less* or *more* but will be able to teach *better*. Professional development can also be tailored to deepen teachers' knowledge of these focal points and connect these ideas in meaningful ways. Assessments can be designed that truly measure students' mastery of core topics rather than survey a broad range of disparate topics, thus allowing for closer monitoring of students' development. At the classroom assessment level, having a smaller number of essential topics will help teachers determine what their students have learned and provide sufficient time to ensure that these topics have been learned deeply enough to use and build on in subsequent years. If state assessments are more focused as well, more detailed information can be gathered for districts and schools on areas for improvement.

Using This Guide in Study Groups or Learning Communities

Many teachers tell us that they did not have an opportunity in school to build sufficient understanding of many topics that they now teach. Therefore our discussion of the grade 5 Focal Points is detailed enough for teachers to begin building such understanding. We suggest that teachers form study groups (such as those in lesson study, mathematics circles, or other learning communities) to read and discuss parts of this volume, to work together to build a deeper understanding of the Focal Points topics, and to plan how to develop such understanding among students by adapting as needed their present grade 5 teaching and learning materials. A helpful approach for other teacher working groups has been to share student insights and questions and to look at student work to understand different ways that students are solving problems, to address errors, and to help move students forward in a progression that fosters both understanding and fluency. Because teachers' lives are busy and demanding, they are better served by concentrating on small chunks of this volume at a time and working through them deeply instead of trying to do too much and getting discouraged. Teachers' learning, like students' learning, is a continuing process, but one that can be very rewarding.

Bringing Focus into the Classroom: Instruction That Builds Understanding and Fluency

Students cannot build understanding in a classroom in which the teacher does all the talking and explaining. Pedagogical principles for classroom teachers that do help students build understanding are outlined in *Principles and Standards for School Mathematics* (NCTM 2000) and the National Research Council reports *Adding It Up* (Kilpatrick, Swafford, and Findell 2001) and *How Students Learn: Mathematics in the Classroom* (Donovan and Bransford 2005). An instructional-progression pedagogical perspective that coordinates the principles from these three sources is outlined in Fuson and Murata (2007). This approach also integrates understanding and fluency. In such an approach, teachers create a nurturing, meaning-making "math talk" community in which students discuss their mathematical thinking and help one another clarify their own thinking, understand and overcome errors, and describe the method they use to solve a problem. Teachers and students assist everyone's learning by coaching one another during such math-talk and during problem solving if needed. Teachers and students model, structure and clarify, instruct or explain, question, and give feedback.

Using mathematical drawings

The use of mathematical drawings during problem solving and explaining of mathematical thinking helps listeners understand the thinking and the explanation of the speaker. The use of mathematical drawings during homework and classwork helps the teacher understand students' thinking and thus provides continual assessment to guide instruction as the teacher addresses issues that arise in such drawings (e.g., errors or interesting mathematical thinking). Mathematical drawings do not show situational details of the real object; such drawings should be done in art class, not in mathematics class. Mathematical drawings focus on the mathematically important features and relationships, such as the quantity and operations, and can use small circles or other simple shapes. These representations can evolve into schematic numerical drawings that show relations or operations. Throughout this volume, we use mathematical drawings that can be produced and understood by students.

Learning phases

The instructional-progression pedagogical perspective that integrates understanding and fluency has four phases for each new topic area. The phases begin by building understanding and then move to emphasizing fluency. For each new mathematics topic, teachers—

a) begin by eliciting students' thinking;

b) teach research-based mathematically desirable and accessible methods that relate easily to standard algorithmic approaches; discuss and repair errors; and ensure that standard approaches are discussed and related to methods that students understand;

c) help students achieve fluency while continuing to build relationships and understanding; and

d) continue cumulative practice occasionally all year so that students remember what they have learned.

Moving to mathematically desirable methods

Eliciting students' thinking when beginning each new topic is important so that the teacher can build on that thinking and modify and extend it as needed. The teacher needs to emphasize sense making by all participants through all four of the phases above. Although some students will develop fairly advanced methods, allowing too much time for students' "invented" methods can leave less-advanced students doing a primitive method that is slow and perhaps error prone for an extended period. Mathematically desirable methods that are generalizable to larger numbers and that use important mathematical aspects of the quantities involved (for example, hundreds, tens, and ones) need to be introduced if they have not arisen from other students or from the instructional program. These methods should also be accessible to students and build on their ways of thinking. We discuss such methods for the grade 5 Focal Points. These methods enable everyone to use a method that they can understand and explain but that is also mathematically desirable.

The standard algorithmic approach

The Focal Points specify topics for which students should achieve fluency with *the standard algorithm*. By this phrase, mathematicians mean *the standard algorithmic approach* that involves certain basic steps and not the specific ways in which numerals are written to show those steps. So, for example, multi-digit multiplication and division involve using the distributive principle to multiply (or divide) places in one number by places in the other number (this concept is discussed and exemplified in the division section). Simpler and more complex ways to write this same standard algorithmic approach are presented later. Each way has disadvantages and advantages, and students can discuss by their relative merits and shortcomings.

Adding It Up (NRC 2001) clarified that in fact no such thing as *the* standard algorithm exists. Many different algorithms (systematic methods of repeated steps for carrying out a computation) have been used over time in the United States, and many different algorithms are used presently in other countries. Students from other countries may bring such written methods into a classroom in the United States. Students from the United States will bring the current common methods learned from experiences at home. All such methods need to be discussed and related to mathematical drawings or other quantities so that all methods can be understood. A student should be allowed to use any method that is mathematically desirable and that the student can explain. Mathematically desirable methods use *the standard algorithmic approach* and therefore meet any state goal that requires use of *the standard algorithm* (these phrases are just alternative words for *the standard algorithmic approach*). Some mathematics programs suggest that students not use the standard algorithm because it often involves a complex way of writing steps, but this method will come from some homes and does need to be included in the class discussion. This view emphasizes that the steps and the meanings underlying the algorithm are the important features, and understanding these—and why they work—is a major focus of the work with the algorithm.

Conceptual prerequisites

Helping all students move rapidly to a mathematically desirable and accessible method requires that they have the conceptual prerequisites for such methods. The teacher may need to build in these prerequisites in advance before introducing the topic. We identify important prerequisites for the grade 5 Focal Points. As the books for grades 3 and 4 are written, an instructional progression of such prerequisites will be available to build coherence across grades in these important learning steps. Meanwhile teacher study groups can work to identify gaps in the knowledge of their students that might need addressing now.

In-depth instructional conversations

During the second learning phase, when multiple methods are discussed and introduced, the math-talk should be an instructional conversation that continually focuses on moving students through learning paths to more-advanced understandings. Such discussions need to identify commonalities and differences and advantages and disadvantages across methods.

Discussions should involve respectful listening to the explanations of others; interrupting to take one's turn explaining without listening to the other explanations should not be permitted. Often a fruitful approach is to go on after two or three explanations to have everyone solve and explain another problem; good methods can be explained on a subsequent problem. Another helpful tactic is to have many students solve at the board while the rest of the class solves at their seats, or use some other method of presenting students' solution methods without wasting class time while students sit doing nothing as other students write their methods on the board.

Many students can understand, relate, and build to fluency more than one method. Thus, they also are following a learning path to increased understanding and fluency even if they began with knowing just one method.

During the third phase of focusing on fluency, the number of problems per class period will increase and the amount of class discussion will decrease. But issues will still arise that need to be discussed and clarified, and the focus on making sense continues during all phases.

Differentiating instruction within whole-class activities

This pedagogical approach, which comes from major national reports and from the NCTM Process Standards, actually allows teachers to differentiate instruction within whole-class activities. Such differentiation is possible because the whole range of student methods from less-advanced to more-advanced are described by students or introduced by the program or by the teacher. The teacher (and, ideally, the mathematics program) helps students move through a learning path to fluency with a mathematically desirable and accessible method or to relating and using two or more such methods.

The three grade 5 Focal Points and their connections appear on the following page.

Curriculum Focal Points and Connections for Grade 5

The set of three curriculum focal points and related connections for mathematics in grade 5 follow. These topics are the recommended content emphases for this grade level. It is essential that these focal points be addressed in contexts that promote problem solving, reasoning, communication, making connections, and designing and analyzing representations.

Grade 5 Curriculum Focal Points	Connections to the Focal Points
Number and Operations and Algebra: Developing an understanding of and fluency with division of whole numbers Students apply their understanding of models for division, place value, properties, and the relationship of division to multiplication as they develop, discuss, and use efficient, accurate, and generalizable procedures to find quotients involving multidigit dividends. They select appropriate methods and apply them accurately to estimate quotients or calculate them mentally, depending on the context and numbers involved. They develop fluency with the standard algorithm, for dividing whole numbers, understand why the procedures work (on the basis of place value and properties of operations), and use them to solve problems. They consider the context in which a problem is situated to select the most useful form of the quotient for the solution, and they interpret it appropriately.	*Algebra:* Students use patterns, models, and relationships as contexts for writing and solving simple equations and inequalities. They create graphs of simple equations. They explore prime and composite numbers and discover concepts related to the addition and subtraction of fractions as they use factors and multiples, including applications of common factors and common multiples. They develop an understanding of the order of operations and use it for all operations. *Measurement:* Students' experiences connect their work with solids and volume to their earlier work with capacity and weight or mass. They solve problems that require attention to both approximation and precision of measurement.
Number and Operations: Developing an understanding of and fluency with addition and subtraction of fractions and decimals Students apply their understandings of fractions and fraction models to represent the addition and subtraction of fractions with unlike denominators as equivalent calculations with like denominators. They apply their understandings of decimal models, place value, and properties to add and subtract decimals. They develop fluency with standard procedures for adding and subtracting fractions and decimals. They make reasonable estimates of fraction and decimal sums and differences. Students add and subtract fractions and decimals to solve problems, including problems involving measurement.	*Data Analysis:* Students apply their understanding of whole numbers, fractions, and decimals as they construct and analyze double-bar and line graphs and use ordered pairs on coordinate grids. *Number and Operations:* Building on their work in grade 4, students extend their understanding of place value to numbers through millions and millionths in various contexts. They apply what they know about multiplication of whole numbers to larger numbers. Students also explore contexts that they can describe with negative numbers (e.g., situations of owing money or measuring elevations above and below sea level.)
Geometry and Measurement and Algebra: Describing three-dimensional shapes and analyzing their properties, including volume and surface area Students relate two-dimensional shapes to three-dimensional shapes and analyze properties of polyhedral solids, describing them by the number of edges, faces, or vertices as well as the types of faces. Students recognize volume as an attribute of three-dimensional space. They understand that they can quantify volume by finding the total number of same-sized units of volume that they need to fill the space without gaps or overlaps. They understand that a cube that is 1 unit on an edge is the standard unit for measuring volume. They select appropriate units, strategies, and tools for solving problems that involve estimating or measuring volume. They decompose three-dimensional shapes and find surface areas and volumes of prisms. As they work with surface area, they find and justify relationships among the formulas for the areas of different polygons. They measure necessary attributes of shapes to use area formulas to solve problems.	

Reprinted from *Curriculum Focal Points for Prekindergarten through Grade 8: A Quest for Coherence* (Reston, Va.: National Council of Teachers of Mathematics, 2006, p. 17).

2 Division

In fifth grade, students continue to develop their understanding of division by building on what they learned in third and fourth grade. The focus in fifth grade is on understanding and gaining fluency with multidigit division problems, including understanding various meanings of remainders in different situations. Accordingly, to understand what students need to know to do well in grade 5, we briefly discuss some of the important ideas that students focus on in grades 3 and 4 that prepare them for multidigit division in grade 5. Of course multiplication is important for all of division, but those ideas will be summarized in the grade 4 book. Grade 4 multidigit multiplication using arrays and area is a particularly important foundation for grade 5 multidigit division.

Progression of ideas about division

Grade 3	Use equal-group, array, and area situations and models to understand and relate the meanings of multiplication and division. Realizing that multiplication and division are inverse operations, view division problems as unknown-factor problems.
	Use lists of multiples (count-by-n lists) for numbers from 1 to 10 to count by a number up to a known product to find the unknown factor in division problems. Count by n up to a known product to obtain the unknown factor by keeping track of the number of counts ($? \times 8 = 32$: 8, 16, 24, 32, so $4 \times 8 = 32$).
	Use properties (commutative, distributive) and known products to find related unknown factors.
Grade 4	Develop fluency with basic division facts (single-digit divisor and quotient).
	Begin to work with division with remainder, especially with "closest facts under" basic facts in preparation for multidigit division. For example, know that when dividing by 6, the closest fact under 50 is $48 \div 6 = 8$ and that 2 will be left when 50 items are divided equally among 6 shares; also $6 \times 8 + 2 = 50$.
	Use division in multiplicative comparison situations (doing so may involve the language of unit fractions). Use division in some combination situations with small numbers (for completeness, because these types of problems are studied in multiplication). Find the unknown factor in these more complex situations as well as in simpler equal-group, array, and area situations.
	Use arrays, areas, and multiplication to understand relationships among division problems involving multiples of 10. Relate division problems involving multiples of 10 (or 100, or 1000) to basic division problems with single-digit factors (e.g., relate $4200 \div 6$ to $42 \div 6$).
Grade 5	Use area drawings and numerical notation to develop and understand methods of division, including the standard algorithmic approach for multidigit dividends and one-digit divisors. The standard algorithmic approach is based on breaking the dividend apart by place value and using the distributive property to find the quotient in pieces by place value.

Grade 5	Use remainders appropriately in solving division story problems. Select the most useful form of a quotient to solve a story problem. Realize that the remainder in a division problem can play different roles in solutions to story problems.
	Understand the standard algorithmic approach for multidigit dividends and two-digit divisors. Examine the important but imperfect roles of estimating and rounding to find the digits in each place of the quotient in such problems, using the same process as that for one-digit divisors.
Grade 6	Understand and develop fluency with division of fractions and decimals.
	Use reasoning about multiplication and division to solve ratio and rate problems.

Types of Problems Solved by Division

Equal-groups situations

In grades 3 and 4, students solve a variety of problems for each of the two types of equal-groups division situations:

- "How many in each group?" or partitive, division situations, and

- "How many groups?" or measurement, division situations.

"How many in each group?" division problems

Suppose 24 students will form 3 equal groups. How many students will be in each group? This is a "how many in each group?" situation that can be shown as

$$24 \div 3 = ?$$

Students can also view this problem as an "unknown factor" multiplication problem, namely, as "3 times how many equals 24?" or

$$3 \times ? = 24,$$

which connects division and multiplication.

"How many groups?" division problems

Suppose 24 students will work in groups of 3. How many groups will there be? This situation is a "how many groups?" situation that can be shown as

$$24 \div 3 = ?$$

Again, students can view this problem as an "unknown factor" multiplication problem, namely, as "how many groups of 3 make 24?" or

$$? \times 3 = 24.$$

They might also be asked, "What number times 3 equals 24?" As before, viewing a division problem as a "missing-factor multiplication problem" connects multiplication and division.

Connecting the two types

Students can use a "dealing out strategy" within an array to see the connection between the two types of division situations ("how many in each group?" and "how many groups?"). For example, as indicated in figure 2.1 to divide 24 objects equally among 3 groups, students can deal 1 object to each group, then deal another object to each group, and so on, until all the objects have been dealt out to the 3 groups, resulting in 8 objects in each group. Every time they deal out 1 object to each group, they make a group of 3 objects. Students can represent this outcome by dividing 24 objects into columns of 3, resulting in 8 groups with 3 objects in each group.

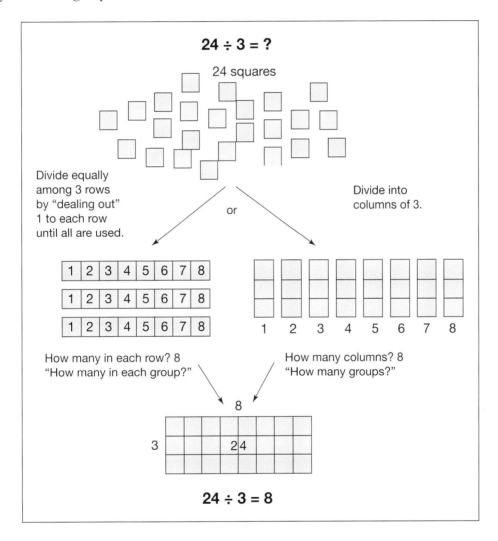

Fig. 2.1. Dividing into 3 groups or groups of 3 to see that 24 ÷ 3 = 8

Division with arrays and area

In grade 3, students solve problem situations involving arrays including arrays of touching squares such as those in figure 2.1. In grades 3 and 4, students also use arrays and areas of rectangles (as well as other visual supports, such as number lines or hundreds grids) to help them reason about multiplication and division. As indicated in figure 2.2, students could view the division problem 36 ÷ 4 = ? as looking for the unknown number of objects along one side of an array when the number of objects in the array and the number of objects along one side of the array are known. Students could also view the division problem as looking for the unknown side length when the area and the length of one side of a rectangle are known.

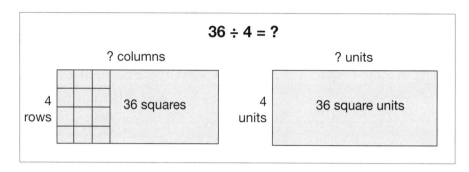

Fig. 2.2. Viewing division as finding an unknown side length

Division with multiplicative comparison situations

In grade 4 students can engage with more complicated multiplication and division situations, including situations involving multiplicative comparison. In these situations, one amount is some number of times as much as another amount. For example, a problem might state that Janet picked 6 times as many apples as her little brother Sean picked. The complex language of multiplicative comparisons is a challenge for students. Students can build on their grade 3 experience with equal-groups situations to solve multiplicative comparison problems by making simple drawings of bars that show the relative sizes of amounts. Making simple drawings (such as the drawing shown in the next set of problems) can help students show and understand multiplicative comparison situations.

Note that multiplicative comparison statements can be rephrased using fractions. For example, if Janet picked 6 times as many apples as Sean, then we can also say that Sean picked 1/6 as many apples as Janet. Although not standard in English, one could also say that Sean picked 1/6 *times* as many apples as Janet. Students should be exposed to multiplicative comparison problems in both whole-number and fraction forms to deepen their understanding of multiplicative comparisons and fractions.

Division Problems in Multiplicative Comparison Situations

1. Janet picked 6 times as many apples as her little brother Sean picked. Janet picked 48 apples. How many apples did Sean pick?

48 Janet: ☐☐☐☐☐☐

___ Sean: ☐

This problem can be rephrased as follows: Sean picked $\frac{1}{6}$ as many apples as Janet picked.

Janet picked 48 apples. How many apples did Sean pick?

2. There were 3 times as many girls as boys at a party. There were 27 girls at the party. How many boys were at the party?
   [Ask students to draw their own picture for this problem.]

Foundations for Understanding Multidigit Division

Using lists of multiples to solve division problems

Grade 3 students often learn multiples (count-bys) by skip-counting. For example, students can skip-count by 5s to list the multiples of 5: 5, 10, 15, 20, …. Multiples are displayed on the rows and columns of the multiplication table. As students skip-count, they often keep track of the multiples on their fingers. For example, when counting by 5s, a student who has 6 fingers raised has counted to 30. Students can apply this knowledge to division. For example, $30 \div 5$ requires counting by 5 up to 30 and seeing (or feeling) that 6 fingers are raised, so $30 \div 5 = 6$ ($? \times 5 = 30$ has been solved as $6 \times 5 = 30$, 6 fives make 30).

Decomposing division problems

For students to become fluent with single-digit multiplication and division as well as to understand why methods of multidigit division work, they must develop skill with decomposing division problems into related division problems.

Relationships among basic facts

In grade 3, students develop fluency with multiplication and division of easier numbers (2s, 5s, 10s, 9s) and explore relationships among basic multiplication facts. These skills prepare students with a foundation of fluency with basic facts (and the associated division facts) to enable them to solve problems with more difficult numbers in grade 4. For example, as indicated with several different representations in figure 2.3a, students might decompose 8×6 as $(5 \times 6) + (3 \times 6)$ (using the distributive property). Students can also think of these drawings as decomposing $48 \div 6$ as $(30 \div 6) + (18 \div 6)$.

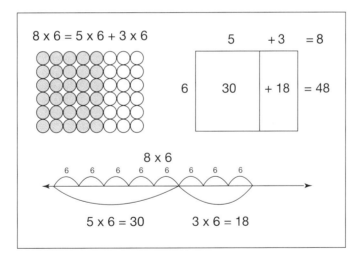

Fig. 2.3a. Decomposing 8×6 or $48 \div 6$

Division problems related by 10, 100, or 1000

Students in grade 4 extend their knowledge of single-digit multiplication by multiplying single-digit numbers by 10, 100, and 1000 and identifying patterns. Fluency with these patterns is required for multi-digit multiplication. Figure 2.3b demonstrates some area and array models that help students understand and generalize the patterns involved with multiplying by 10, 100, and 1000.

$3 \times 2 = 6$

$3 \times 20 = 60 \quad [3 \times 20 = 3 \times 2 \times 10 = 6 \times 10 = 60]$

$30 \times 20 = 600 \quad [30 \times 20 = 3 \times 2 \times 10 \times 10 = 6 \times 100 = 600]$

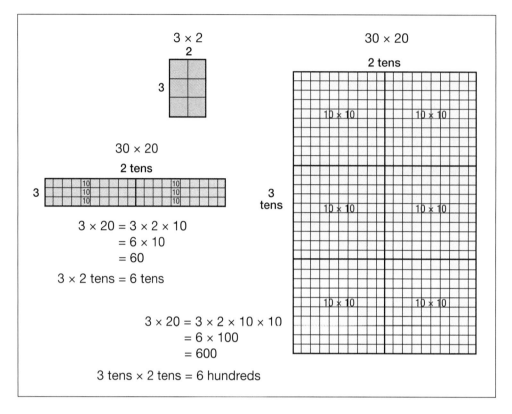

Fig. 2.3b. Multiplication with tens

Students can use their knowledge about patterns associated with multiplying by 10, 100, and 1000 to solve division problems. Knowing and understanding connections among division problems that are related by 10, 100, or 1000 are of special importance for efficient mental calculation and for understanding efficient methods of multidigit division methods. For example, as illustrated in figures 2.3b and 2.4, Students can think about arrays and area models; objects bundled in groups of 10, 100, and 1000; and $1, $10, and $100 bills, students to see a relationship or pattern among division problems dealing with multiples of 10, 100, or 1000. In figure 2.4, students see representations of groups of 10 or 100 and can see the relationship among the division problems

$$6 \div 3 = 2,$$
$$60 \div 3 = 20,$$
$$600 \div 3 = 200$$

and

$$6 \div 2 = 3,$$
$$60 \div 20 = 3,$$
$$600 \div 200 = 3.$$

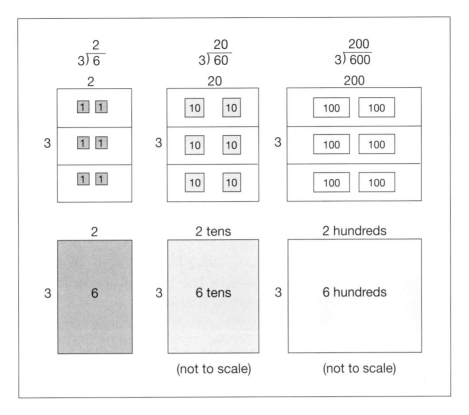

Fig. 2.4. Division problems related by 10 and 100

Working toward developing efficient methods of division

Exploring multigit division methods

Some students initially solve a multidigit division problem by making a list of multiples of the divisor. For example, a student might use a list like the one on the left in figure 2.5 to explain why 112 ÷ 7 = 16. Others use repeated doubling to generate multiples, as shown on the right in figure 2.5, and then select from those multiples to multiply or divide to build up a known product so as to find the unknown factor (this method is sometimes called the *Russian peasant method*). For example, to use the repeated doubling list to calculate 98 ÷ 7, a student can look for entries on the right of the list that add to 98. A student might first add 56 + 28 = 84 and then notice that 14 more makes 98, so that 98 ÷ 7 = 8 + 4 + 2 = 14.

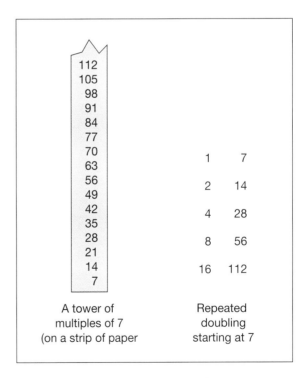

Fig. 2.5. Multiples of 7

However, listing multiples is primitive and time-consuming, and division problems with larger dividends, such as 476 ÷ 7, become too tedious to solve by making a list of multiples of 7 all the way to 476. Furthermore, these methods do not use place values to build up the places in the unknown factor as rapidly as possible, as used in standard algorithms. Students need to move on to using multiples of 10 to understand and take advantage of our base-ten place-value system.

Using multiples of 10 to improve efficiency and increase place-value understanding

Students can apply their previous work on multiplication and division problems involving multiples of 10 or 100 to strings of related multiplication and division problems, as in the next sets of strings of related problems.

Strings of Related Problems Involving Multiples of 10 and 100:
Playing with Place Values in the Unknown Factor

For each set, give students a few minutes to solve the problems. Ask students to explain the strategies they used. Have students who cannot solve mentally make a drawing. For example, the array drawings below could help students see how 40 ÷ 4, 80 ÷ 4, 120 ÷ 4, and 124 ÷ 4 are related.

Notice also that problems involving division by 25 can be thought of in terms of money. For example, 150 ÷ 25 = 6 because 6 quarters make $1.50, which is 150 cents.

40 ÷ 4	100 ÷ 25	900 ÷ 9	2100 ÷ 21
80 ÷ 4	150 ÷ 25	1800 ÷ 9	8400 ÷ 21
120 ÷ 4	200 ÷ 25	1809 ÷ 9	8421 ÷ 21
124 ÷ 4	600 ÷ 25	1818 ÷ 9	8436 ÷ 21

Students need practice with the simple division patterns involving multiples of 10 and 100 and the simple related division problems that use those patterns. With such experiences, students can then solve 434 ÷ 7 by building up tens multiples of 7, as on the left in figure 2.6, or by successively subtracting multiples of 7, as shown on the right in figure 2.6.

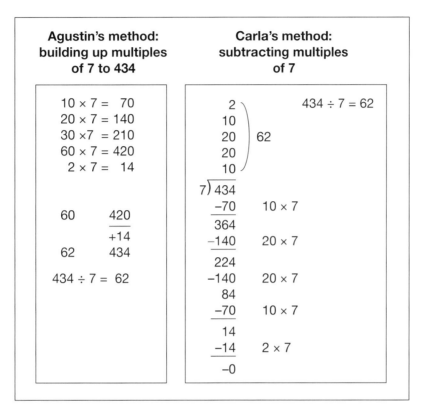

Fig. 2.6. Early methods that students develop to solve division problems

Notice that both methods in figure 2.6 implicitly involve the distributive property and build up partial quotients for each place value. Namely, on the left, 434 is decomposed as

$$434 = 420 + 14 = 60 \times 7 + 2 \times 7 = (60 + 2) \times 7 = 62 \times 7,$$

and on the right, 434 is decomposed as

$$434 = 10 \times 7 + 20 \times 7 + 20 \times 7 + 10 \times 7 + 2 \times 7 = (10 + 20 + 20 + 10 + 2) \times 7 = 62 \times 7.$$

Explorations such as those in figure 2.6 can contribute to students' understanding of division, but using such small numbers and building up each place of the factor in such small increments is slow and tedious. Students do need to learn to generate close factors for each place rather than continue this introductory approach.

The Standard Algorithmic Approach to Division

Most people understand "the standard division algorithm" to mean the specific way of recording the numerical steps of the long-division procedure that is shown on the far right in figures 2.7 and 2.10. From a purely mathematical perspective, where or how the steps of an algorithm are recorded does not matter, because the steps themselves constitute the algorithm. But from the perspective of learning and understanding, where or how the steps of an algorithm are recorded can be crucially important. We therefore use the term *standard algorithmic approach* for the collection of all sensible ways of showing or recording the steps of the usual division algorithm. This perspective allows students to use and record the division algorithm in ways that make sense to them. This perspective also recognizes that the steps and the logic of an algorithm are at the heart of the algorithm, not the particular method of recording it. In this section we describe some pictorial methods that depict the standard algorithmic approach to division, and we describe how they are related to the common way of writing this algorithm.

The use of place value and the distributive property

In the standard algorithmic approach to division, one finds the unknown factor (the quotient) place by place, forming partial quotients by using the distributive property to break the dividend apart by place value. The process starts from the place of highest value in the dividend and proceeds to the lower places by successively dividing the amount at a given place and unbundling the remainder to put with the amount in the next lower place.

Figure 2.7 shows a way to represent calculating $78 \div 3$ using one pictorial version of the standard algorithmic approach to division. The dividend 78 is decomposed into 7 tens and 8 ones. Division proceeds by first dividing the tens, then unbundling the remaining ten so that it can be combined with the ones, and finally dividing the ones. The net effect is that 78 is decomposed as

$$78 = 20 \times 3 + 6 \times 3 = (20 + 6) \times 3 = 26 \times 3.$$

Therefore $78 \div 3 = 26$.

Notice that students could also solve $78 \div 3$ mentally by noticing that 3 quarters make 75 cents and 3 more cents make 78 cents, so $78 \div 3 = 25 + 1 = 26$.

Students' array drawings

Arrays are a powerful model for grade 4 multidigit multiplication because they show very clearly the partial products made by the tens and ones. These experiences provide important grounding for visualizing multidigit division with arrays or areas in which the product and one side are known but the other side is not known (for example, as indicated at the top of fig. 2.8). Throughout the steps, students can think either of the total numbers of things (seen in the expanded notation in the middle of fig. 2.8) or of the values of the places (seen in the place-value digit notation on the bottom).

Figures 2.9 and 2.10 show a larger division problem worked out with an area drawing and the place-value-digit notation. This place-value notation is the current most common way of recording the standard algorithmic approach, but it is often taught and learned just as a rote procedure with single digits. The use of the place-value array drawing as in figures 2.9 and 2.10 shows the meanings of the digits as their place-value quantities. Such meanings need to be elicited and discussed when teaching and learning division. Also, discussing the place-value notation (as shown in fig. 2.10) can be helpful in ensuring that students understand the place values involved.

To use an array drawing, students view a division problem as the problem of finding an unknown side length when the area of a rectangle and one of its side lengths are known, as indicated at the top of figure 2.9. The total length of the unknown side length is found in stages starting at the place of highest value and proceeding to places of lower value, as indicated at the bottom of figure 2.9 and shown step by step in figure 2.10a.

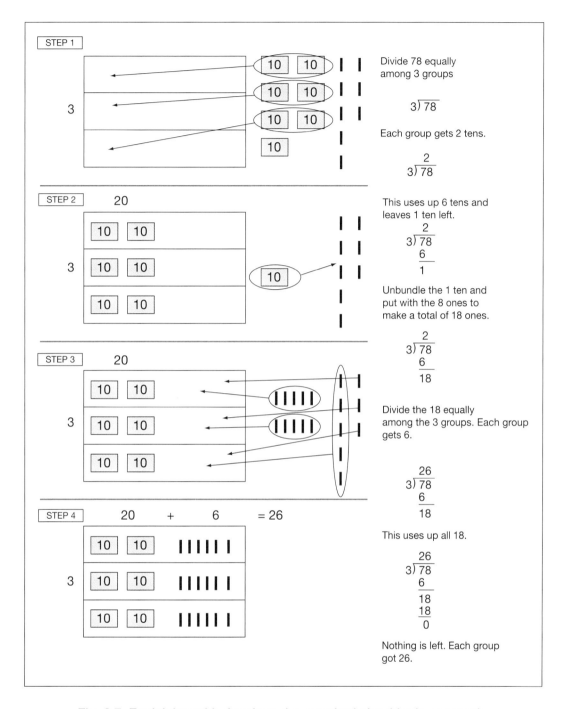

Fig. 2.7. Explaining with drawings the standard algorithmic approach using an equal-groups model

Students can also record the place-value components of 1721 within the rectangle as 1000, 700, 20, 1 instead of as 1 Th, 7 H, 2 T (see fig. 2.10b). This expanded notation recording shows the running total of all the things still to be divided in each step. Using this notation, students can "underguess" or "underestimate" quotients, although they need move to close factors and not continue to use the early methods shown in figure 2.6 (Agustin's and Carla's), in which the build-up for each place is very slow.

Students need to solve a variety of types of multidigit division problems, including all the types discussed previously.

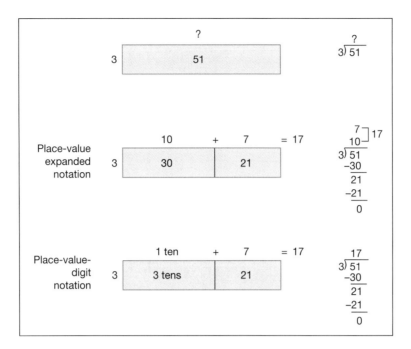

Fig. 2.8. Showing division with an array and two numerical recordings

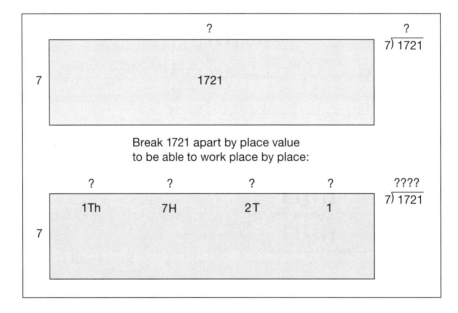

Fig. 2.9. Viewing a division problem as an unknown-side-length problem

Common errors with the standard division algorithmic approach written in place-value-digit form

One difficulty that students face is what to do when zeros are encountered. Thinking about the meanings of the place values and using estimation to determine whether answers are reasonable can help.

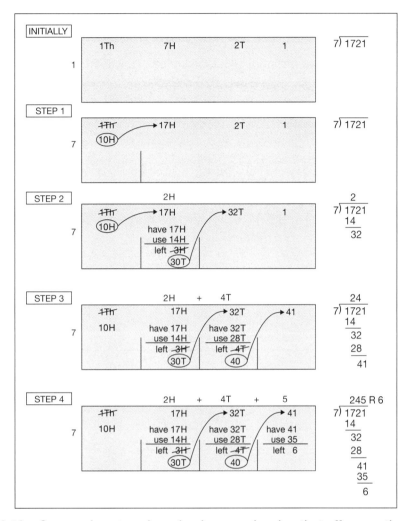

Fig. 2.10a. Successive steps in a simple array drawing that offers another way to record the standard algorithmic approach to division

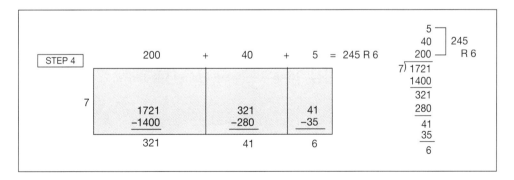

Fig. 2.10b. An expanded division algorithm shown pictorially and in standard notation

A zero can be encountered in the dividend, such as in 805 ÷ 3, as in case A of figure 2.11. In this case, students may be confused about what to do with the 0 in the dividend. They should realize that the remaining 2 hundreds must be unbundled to make 20 tens. In this case, because of the 0 in the dividend, no additional tens are available to combine with the 20 tens. Students also should realize that 2 cannot be the correct quotient because the quotient must be at least 200.

Problem Solving with Division

1. A sidewalk is 5 feet wide and has area 1430 square feet. How long is the sidewalk?

2. Tara collected 3 times as many cans as Robert. If Tara collected 78 cans, how many cans did Robert collect? Santiago collected 4 times as many cans as Carla. If Carla collected 48 cans, how many cans did Santiago collect?

Note: When solving these kinds of problems, students might like to draw pictures like the one below to show the relative sizes of quantities.

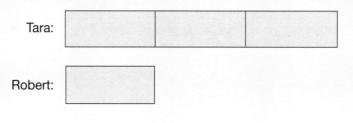

Tara:

Robert:

Case A	Case B	Case C
2 3)805 6 2	2 3)65 6 0	3 14)4314 42 11
What to do about the 0?	Stop now because of the 0?	Stop now because 11 is less than 14?
2 hundreds = 20 tens.	No, there are still 5 ones left.	No, it is 11 tens, so there are still 110 + 4 = 114 left.

Fig. 2.11. Common difficulties with the place-value-digit form of the standard division algorithmic approach. Thinking about the meanings of the place values can help.

A zero can be encountered as a remainder in an intermediate step, such as at the first step in 65 ÷ 3, as in case B of figure 2.11. Students should realize that they are not yet done, because 5 ones are still left and they have not yet determined the ones place of the quotient. Students also should realize that 2 cannot be the correct quotient because the quotient must be at least 20.

Zeros in the quotient can also pose difficulty for students. In case C of figure 2.11, the tens digit in the quotient of 4314 ÷ 14 is zero. Students may think they should stop when they have only 11 tens remaining and they are dividing by 14. Students should also see that 3 cannot be the answer because 3 times 14 is only 42, which is much less than 4314.

Emphasizing multidigit division as the related multiplication with an unknown factor (known factor × unknown factor = product) can help students use their multiplication knowledge to overcome errors in division.

Estimating for two-digit divisors

When the divisor in a division problem has two or more digits, estimation at each step becomes especially important. Rounding numbers is not always sufficient to find the correct digit in a quotient. For example, in the first step of the division problem 923 ÷ 18, the student might round 18 to 20 and 92 (tens) to 90 (tens) and figure that the tens digit of the quotient ought to be 4. The correct digit, however, is 5. A difficulty with the place-value-digit notation for the numerical computation is that the exact maximum number of times the divisor goes into the quotient at that step must be found. When the student finds that the remainder is greater than 18, the student will have to change the 4 in the tens place of the quotient to a 5 and multiply again. The expanded notation method shown in figure 2.10b allows students to use the 40 and continue the division process by writing a 10 above the 40, as shown in figure 2.12.

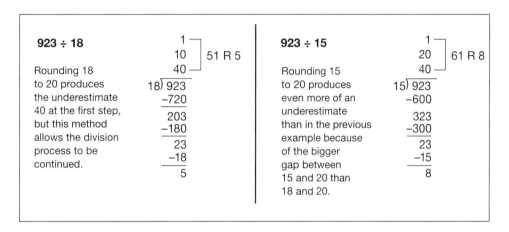

Fig. 2.12. Expanded notation method allows for underestimates in division.

Similarly, in the first step of the division problem 839 ÷ 23, the student might round 23 to 20 and 83 (tens) to 80 (tens) and decide that the tens digit of the quotient should be 4, although 4 turns out to be too high so 3 must be used. In such situations, both numerical versions require doing that step over again. Discussing both kinds of rounding problems with students is helpful so that they understand that such difficulty is inherent in the division process and is not an error on their part. Students also can be helped to see that such difficulties are more likely when rounding is far than when it is close. For example, as seen in figure 2.12, in the division problems 923 ÷ 18 and 923 ÷ 15, the bigger gap in rounding the divisor 15 to 20 than rounding the divisor 18 to 20 produces more of an underestimate in the first partial quotient (only 600 instead of 720 to be subtracted from 923). In the example on the right in figure 2.12 (923 ÷ 15), the second step needs a next partial quotient 20, whereas the 923 ÷ 18 needs a second partial quotient of only 10.

Division with Remainder

In fourth grade, students begin to work with remainders in division. Of special importance in preparation for multidigit division are processes for finding the "closest basic fact under" a number. For example, when dividing by 8, the closest basic division fact under 37 is 32 ÷ 8 = 4. Students learn that the notation 37 ÷ 8 = 4 R 5 means that when 37 objects are divided equally among 8 groups, the largest whole number of objects that can be put in each group is 4, and 5 objects are left over (or when 37 objects are divided into groups of 8, the largest whole number of groups that can be made is 4, and 5 objects are left over). The

---

More Problem Solving with Division

1. The teacher has 75 sheets of graph paper. Then she gets 65 more sheets of graph paper. If the teacher shares the graph paper equally among her 27 students, how many sheets of graph paper does each student get?

2. At a soda factory, cans of soda are put into 6-packs. The 6-packs are then put into cases. Each case holds 4 six-packs. There are 3237 cans of soda at the factory. How many cases will that quantity make? Will any 6-packs be left over? Will any sodas that aren't in a 6-pack be left over?

Notice that these problems are multiple-step situations. Grade 5 students should have experiences solving such problems as well as solving single-step problems.

---

statement $37 \div 8 = 4$ R 5 can also be recorded with the equation $8 \times 4 + 5 = 37$, which clearly indicates that the remainder was part of the original dividend 37. Students practice evaluating expressions of the form $8 \times 4 + 5$. Then students practice the reverse, finding the "closest basic fact under" a number, which will help them with division involving dividends over 100 in grade 5.

In fifth grade students work more extensively with remainders and work with a variety of situations and problems that involve remainders. Students need to experience these situations and decide what to do with the remainder to answer the question that was posed.

What to Do with the Remainder?

1. There are 86 pencils to be divided equally among 9 students. How many pencils will each student get?

2. Each car holds 7 people. How many cars will be needed to take 45 students and teachers on a field trip?

3. At a bakery, muffins are put in packages of 6. There are 50 muffins. After the muffins are put in packages, the workers get to eat any muffins that are left. How many muffins do the workers get?

4. Eleven cups of flour must be divided equally into 3 parts. How much flour is in each part?

5. $11 is to be divided equally among 3 people. How much does each person get?

6. Quint needs to cut a rope that is 11 feet long into 3 equal pieces. How long should each piece be?

---

1. *Ignore the remainder.* In problem 1 above, the remaining pencils can simply be ignored to answer the question (maybe the teacher will save the remaining pencils for later use).

2. *Add 1 to the quotient.* In problem 2, the solution to the division problem $45 \div 7$ is 6, remainder 3, which means that 6 cars will be full, but the remaining 3 people will need another car. So the answer to problem 2 is that 7 cars will be needed.

3. *The remainder is the answer.* In problem 3, the remainder of the division problem $50 \div 6$ is the answer to the question.

As problems 2 and 3 show, the solution to a story problem is not necessarily the same as the solution to a related division problem. In fifth grade students solve division problems that have mixed-number or decimal solutions, such as problems 4 and 5 above, or that are best answered using two different units, such as problem 6.

4. *Mixed-number answer.* In problem 4, each part can first receive 3 whole cups of flour, using up 9 cups. When the remaining 2 cups of flour are divided equally among the 3 parts, each part receives another 2/3 cup (see the fraction chapter for a discussion about the connection between division and fractions). So in all, each part contains $3^2/_3$ cups of flour.

5. *Decimal answer.* Like problem 4, problem 5 also involves the division problem 11 ÷ 3, but in this example, a decimal answer, namely, $3.66, better fits the situation (and the extra pennies can be given away).

6. *Using two units in the answer.* Like problems 4 and 5, problem 6 also involves the division problem 11 ÷ 3. Although to say that each piece of rope is $3^2/_3$ feet long is correct, when one actually measures the rope, a more useful answer is that each piece is 3 feet, 8 inches long.

Equivalent Division Problems as Transitions to Ratio and Rate

Students can begin to see division within the context of ratio situations by solving such problems as the Sharing Tickets Problem that follows.

Sharing Tickets Problem

100 tickets were shared equally among 4 students; 200 tickets were shared among 8 other students; and 300 tickets were shared among 12 other students. Did every student get the same number of tickets? How can you tell? How many tickets did each student get?

Division problems that have the same solution are called *equivalent*. By thinking about relationships between quantities, and by drawing arrays or area pictures, such as those shown in figure 2.13, students can explain why 100 ÷ 4, 200 ÷ 8, and 300 ÷ 12 are equivalent division problems.

Some teachers and students like to record dividends and divisors of equivalent division problems in a ratio table, such as the one in table 2.1. We can think of this table as showing equivalent rates, namely, rates that are equivalent to 25 tickets per 1 person.

Table 2.1
Example of a Ratio Table

# tickets	25	100	200	300
# people	1	4	8	12

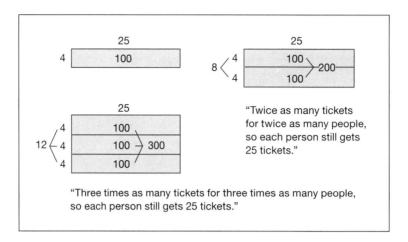

Fig. 2.13. Showing that 100 ÷ 4, 200 ÷ 8, and 300 ÷ 12 are equivalent

In general, given any division problem, we can multiply or divide the dividend and the divisor by the same number (other than 0), and the new division problem has the same solution. In sixth grade this fact about equivalent division problems allows students to solve division problems that involve decimals by replacing the problems with equivalent division problems that involve only whole numbers. For example, if we multiply both the dividend and the divisor of 7.2 ÷ 2.4 by 10, then we get an equivalent division problem, 72 ÷ 24, which involves only whole numbers.

3 Addition and Subtraction of Fractions and Decimals

In fifth grade students use their understanding of fractions and decimals to add and subtract decimals; to develop understanding of, and fluency with, standard procedures for adding and subtracting fractions and decimals; to solve problems that require adding and subtracting fractions and decimals; and to make reasonable estimates of fraction and decimal sums and differences. In this chapter we discuss the central fraction and decimal understandings that lead up to fraction and decimal addition and subtraction and must be developed in grades 3, 4, and 5.

Fractions and decimals use different systems of notation, which create differences in how addition and subtraction are carried out. But the same fundamental idea is used for both: add (or subtract) like units. For fractions, the units are the unit fractions, namely,

$$\frac{1}{2}, \ \frac{1}{3}, \ \frac{1}{4}, \ \frac{1}{5}, \dots$$

For decimals, the units are the unit decimal fractions,

$$0.1 = \frac{1}{10}, \ 0.01 = \frac{1}{100}, \ 0.001 = \frac{1}{1000}, \dots,$$

which are those unit fractions whose denominators are powers of ten. Because the differences in notation create such different ways of working with fractions and decimals, we first discuss fractions and decimals separately and then discuss links between fractions and decimals.

Progression of ideas related to fraction and decimal addition and subtraction, and the connections between fractions and decimals

Grade 3	Understand unit fractions as equal divisions of a whole.
	Understand that a fraction is a sum of unit fractions.
	Understand that for unit fractions, a greater denominator gives a smaller unit fraction because more of them are in the same whole. Fold fraction strips and see fraction bars to visualize this relationship.
	Understand how to compare and order fractions that already have the same numerator (e.g., 2/3, 2/5) or the same denominator (e.g., 4/5, 2/5).
	See equivalent fractions in fraction strips, fraction bars, and number lines.

Grade 4	Understand how and why to add, subtract, and compare fractions less than 1 that have the same denominator.
	Understand how and why to find equivalent fractions to add, subtract, and compare fractions less than 1 that have different denominators.
	Understand decimal notation as an extension of the base-ten system.
	Understand how to connect fractions and decimals in simple (limited) cases.
Grade 5	Develop fluency with adding, subtracting, and comparing fractions and mixed numbers with the same or with different denominators.
	Develop fluency with adding, subtracting, and comparing decimals alone and with whole numbers.
	Understand the connection between fractions and division, that is, $A \div B = A/B$.
Grades 6 and 7	Understand how to use division to write a fraction as a decimal.
Grade 8 or later	Understand why the decimal representations of fractions must either terminate or repeat and why terminating and repeating decimals can be written as fractions.

Fractions

In third and fourth grade, students focus on the meaning and uses of fractions. They use models (pictures), including such length models as fraction bars, to compare and order fractions. To give a more complete picture of the mathematical terrain, this section looks into some of the important fraction ideas that underlie learning about fraction addition and subtraction, which is a focus in grade 5.

Definition of fraction

In third grade, students begin to focus on fractions. The need for numbers other than whole numbers can be made motivating for students by using measurement contexts. For example, when the contents of a bottle of juice is poured into identical cups, the juice may fill several cups completely, but may fill only a part of the last cup. To describe the total number of cups of juice that was in the bottle, a whole number does not suffice.

What are fractions? The unit fractions,

$$\frac{1}{2}, \frac{1}{3}, \frac{1}{4}, \frac{1}{5},$$

and so on—namely, fractions that have numerator 1—are building blocks for all fractions and are a good starting point in defining fractions. Unit fractions are formed by dividing a whole into equal parts. To show 1/4 of something, divide the thing into 4 equal parts. The amount formed by one of those parts is 1/4 of the thing. In other words, an amount is 1/4 of a thing if 4 copies of the amount make the whole thing. See figure 3.1. Other unit fractions can be defined in the same way.

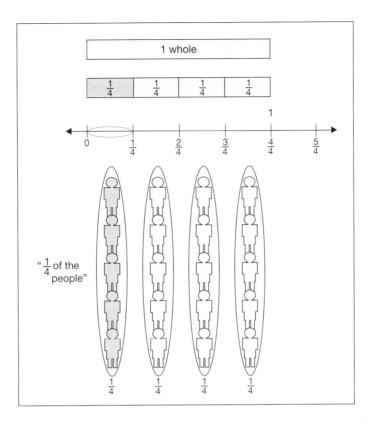

Fig. 3.1. When something is divided into 4 equal parts, the amount formed by one of those parts is 1/4 of the thing.

Nonunit fractions, such as 3/4, can be defined in terms of unit fractions. To show 3/4 of something, show the amount formed by 3 parts, each of which is 1/4 of the thing (see fig. 3.2a). Notice that when we say "three-fourths," we first say the *number* of parts we are considering (here: 3 parts) and then say the *size* of the parts (here: each part is 1/4 of the whole thing). Fractions might be easier to grasp if we first said the size of the parts and then said the number of those parts that we are considering. In some languages, the fraction 3/4 is read as "out of 4 parts, take 3," so that the size of the parts is indicated first and then the number of parts being considered is stated. Another confusing aspect of the way we say fractions in English is that most of the words we use to indicate the size of a fractional part, as in "a third," "a fourth," and so on, are the same as the ordinal words we use to indicate position, as in "third in line," "fourth in line," and the like. Students can say fractions using the meaningful language (e.g., say 3/4 as "out of 4 parts, take 3") along with the English fraction term ("three-fourths") to help initial understanding of fractions.

Other nonunit fractions can be defined in the same way that 3/4 was defined from 1/4. In other words, all fractions are built from putting unit fractions together. In general, a/b of something is the amount formed by a parts, each of which is $1/b$ of the thing.

Special care must be taken to help students make sense of improper fractions, in which the numerator (the top number in a fraction) is greater than the denominator (the bottom number in a fraction). For example, 5/4 of a cup of water is the amount formed by 5 parts, each of which is 1/4 of a cup. Also see figure 3.2b. However, an important point to emphasize to students is that the term *improper fraction* is unfortunate. Improper fractions are just regular fractions that happen to be greater than 1.

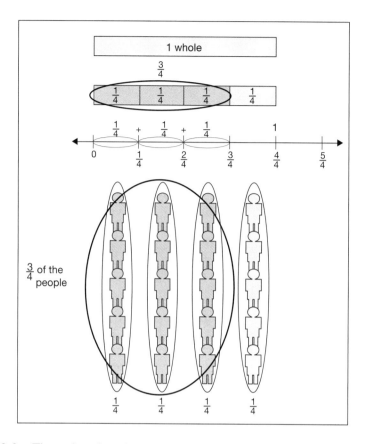

Fig. 3.2a. Three-fourths of something is the amount formed by 3 parts, each of which is 1/4 of the thing.

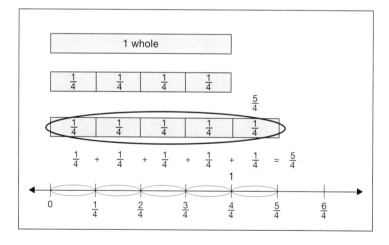

Fig. 3.2b. The improper fraction 5/4

Fractions are related to a whole

Understanding that a fraction is related to a whole is central to understanding fractions. A fraction of a thing is related to the thing—and the "thing" does not have to be a single contiguous entity—it can be a collection of objects or it can be some quantity. As numbers, fractions are related to the whole.

Figure 3.3a shows that a fraction depends on the whole because 1/2 of a large thing is not the same quantity as 1/2 of a small thing. Figure 3.3b shows that a given quantity can represent different fractions depending on what the whole is.

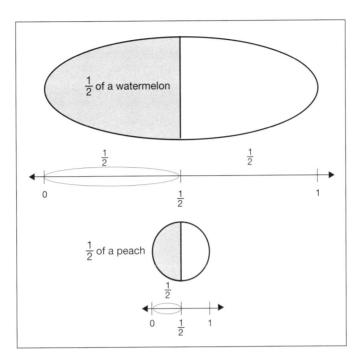

Fig. 3.3a. Fractions depend on the whole: 1/2 of a large amount is a different quantity than 1/2 of a smaller amount.

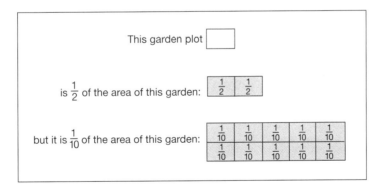

Fig. 3.3b. Fractions depend on the whole: a quantity can be 1/2 of one whole but 1/10 of another whole.

The next problems can be used to focus students' attention on the relationship between fractions and the associated whole.

Fractions That Add to One Whole

1. Tyler has a long submarine sandwich that is divided into 5 equal pieces. Tyler decides to eat some of his sandwich now, and some later. On each fifths bar, circle two groups made of some number of fifths to show a fraction of the sandwich that Tyler could eat now and a fraction he could eat later. Then write the equation next to each bar to show how he split the sandwich.

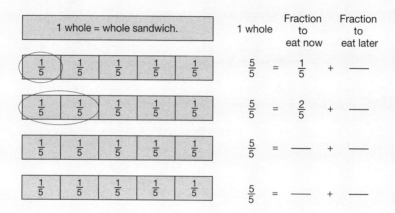

2. At the mall, Anna spent $\frac{2}{7}$ of her money and saved the rest. What fraction of her money did Anna save?

Problems like problem 1 of the activity "Fractions That Add to One Whole," in which students write addend pairs for 1 whole, can help students overcome two typical errors. First, some students see a picture like that in figure 3.3c as 2/3 because they see 2 parts and 3 parts. Seeing two parts of a drawing is easier than seeing a part and a total because the part is embedded in the total. Labeling each part with its unit fraction helps students see and keep in mind the total of 5 parts. Showing the whole above the fractional part is also important to remind students that fractions are related to a whole.

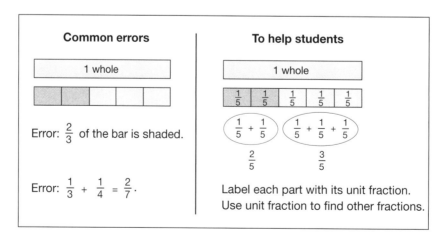

Fig. 3.3c. Common errors and ways to help

Second, when students add fractions, a typical error is to add the tops and bottoms, as in

$$\frac{1}{3} + \frac{1}{4} = \frac{2}{7},$$

which is incorrect. Early experience writing addend pairs, as in problem 1 of the activity "Fractions That Add to One Whole," emphasizes that the denominator stays the same and just the numerators are added (when adding fractions that have the same denominator).

Being clear about what the whole is when depicting improper fractions and mixed numbers is especially important because an amount greater than 1 whole will probably be assumed to be the whole unless otherwise specified.

The underlying whole of a fraction need not be a single contiguous whole but can also be a set of things or a quantity. When finding a fraction of a set or a quantity, students solve "how many in each group?" division problems. For example, if 12 pencils are in a box, then to find 1/3 of the pencils, students must divide the 12 pencils into 3 equal groups. One-third of the pencils is the amount in one of those groups, namely, 4 pencils. Numerically, finding a fraction of a set corresponds to fraction multiplication. For example,

$$\frac{2}{3} \text{ of } 12 \text{ is } \frac{2}{3} \cdot 12.$$

So students' experience with finding a fraction of a set should generally be limited to pictorial examples or examples involving unit fractions until they begin to study fraction multiplication (which is a focus in sixth grade).

Fractions of Sets

1. Shade $\frac{1}{8}$ of the rectangle.

2. Shade $\frac{3}{8}$ of the rectangle.

3. Mr. Fennell has a box of 24 pieces of fruit. $\frac{1}{3}$ are oranges, $\frac{1}{6}$ are grapefruit, and the rest are tangerines.

How many oranges are there?
How many grapefruit are there?
How many tangerines are there?

Representing fractions

Students need experience with situational and visual representations of fractions to understand what fractions are and how to compute with them. A helpful approach is to see various shapes of wholes equally divided to make fractional parts. But subdividing circles equally into odd numbers of parts is difficult, as is working with parts from circles to find equivalent fractions for adding and subtracting unlike fractions. Rectangles work better, but students then have to focus on two dimensions. Length models are easy to visualize and to divide and subdivide equally. We therefore use length models here.

Many approaches to fractions begin by having students fold fraction strips to make various fractions. Students can learn important concepts if they reflect on and discuss such experiences. They can see that by folding strips into more pieces, the pieces get smaller. They practice the basic idea of fractions: that 1/4 is one of four equal parts of some whole. Their difficulty in folding 3 or 5 equal parts may lead some to tear off the extra piece they have after making 3 equal pieces, thus giving an opportunity to discuss that fractions to be compared must be parts of the same whole (but they have just shortened the whole). Students' fraction strips are not a good basis for further detailed work with fractions, however, because they are difficult to lay out to make the comparisons one wants to make for various operations and are hard to split into multiple equal portions on the same strip. Better models for such tasks are drawings of fraction bars that can be produced in class and that may appear on workbook pages. We have used such drawings here. Students' drawings do not have to be totally accurate (the 1/4ths should be roughly but do not need to be exactly 4 equal parts). Labels for important parts of the drawing can clarify the drawing. Students do not always have to draw a long 1 bar first and then divide it equally unless that 1 whole is given as a particular length. They can draw a unit-fraction bar (e.g., draw a short 1/5 bar) and then build up the total fraction by making more such bars after it. This approach helps to emphasize that 4/5 (for example) is made from four of the unit 1/5 bars.

Fraction bars are more concrete than are number lines because the parts of a bar can be labeled in the middle to make their parts clear. Number lines consist of a line that is divided by small vertical line segments that are labeled to show the total length from the zero point. A number line is a length model in which the unit fractions are the equal lengths. But the lengths get "lost" visually, and the eye is drawn to the labeled points. Because students' experiences for most of their lives are based on count models (counts of things in the world), they often try to use the number line as a count model, making different kinds of errors. If they draw a fraction on a number line without any start and finish segments, they may make an error like the first error shown in figure 3.3d, omitting the 0 point and having one too few points (this drawing could just be considered incomplete, but many students who make such a drawing do not even know that they need a 0 point). If students draw a fraction on a number line that already has the 0 and 1 places labeled, they may make 4 points to show the four fourths, as in the second error shown in figure 3.3d, having one too many points.

When using number lines, it is helpful to draw thin ovals around the fraction lengths to be sure that students are focusing on those lengths. We have done so here (e.g., see figs. 3.2a, 3.2b, and 3.3a). The errors that students make with number lines and the need to look at the fraction lengths should be discussed with students. In later grades, when graphing on the coordinate plane, students may focus on points as well as on lengths for certain kinds of problems. But they need to focus on the lengths in numbers lines if they are to make sense of number-line operations on fractions in elementary school.

Because of the difficulty of number-line visualizations, fraction bars might be used for initial understandings of fractions and for comparison, addition, and subtraction with like and unlike fractions. Older students examining multiplication and division of fractions might use number lines because they do need to become familiar with this mathematical representation and overcome their errors in using it. At this time they would be helped by relating number lines as fraction models to their other uses in rulers and

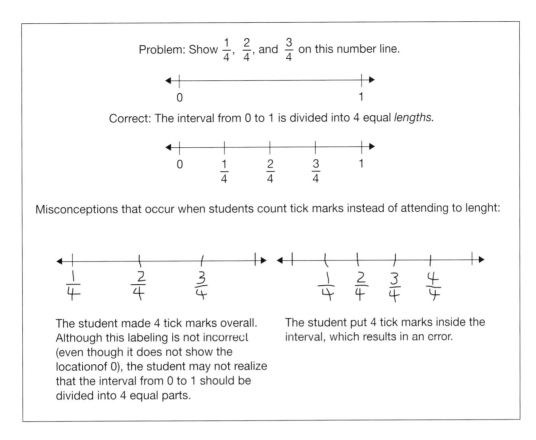

Fig. 3.3d. Errors students make with fractions on number lines when they do not attend to length but focus on numbers of tick marks

in scales for graphing. These representations are all the same, and all of them use length. Rulers used at a given grade should have only the fractional marks for the fractions used at that grade level. The standard U.S. inch ruler divided into sixteenths is too complex for grades 2, 3, and 4. Grade 2 students first measuring length need to have rulers with whole-number units only, although they will deal conceptually with halves as they round to the nearest unit length. Grade 3 students could measure with a ruler having halves and fourths, and grade 4 students could measure using eighths. Of course tenths, hundredths, and thousandths are especially important in connection with metersticks and other metric rulers. These partitionings are discussed in the section on decimals.

Comparing fractions

Given two fractions, which one is greater? A good first case for students is to consider this question for unit fractions.

Comparing unit fractions

As figure 3.4 shows, the greater the denominator, the smaller the unit fraction, because when a whole is divided into more parts, each part is smaller than when the same whole is divided into fewer parts.

A common misconception is the belief that the bigger the denominator, the bigger the fraction. For example, many students think that 1/8 is greater than 1/7. They reason that since 8 is bigger than 7, something with 8 parts must be bigger than something with 7 parts. Students must be aware that when we compare two fractions, we refer to the same underlying whole. Students must also be aware that a

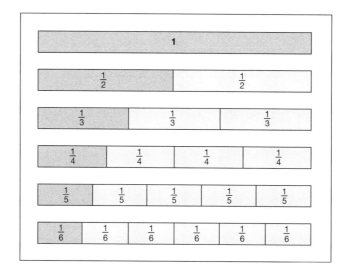

Fig. 3.4. The greater the denominator, the smaller the unit fraction.

number plays a different role when it is in the numerator of a fraction than when it is in the denominator, just as they must be aware that the digits in a whole number play different roles, so that the 7 in 5786 stands for a larger amount than the 8 does. Students need repeated experiences remembering the meaning of a unit fraction and seeing a figure like figure 3.4 to overcome their automatic response that is based on thinking about whole numbers. A real-world situation that helps is asking, "Would you rather have

$$\frac{1}{4} \text{ or } \frac{1}{5}$$

of a pizza?" Students realize that a pizza shared equally among only 4 people gives each person more pizza than if the same pizza were shared equally among 5 people.

Comparing fractions that have the same numerator

Once students understand the role of the denominator in comparing unit fractions, they can see that more generally, if two fractions have the same numerator, then the one with the larger denominator is smaller. For example, 3/8 is greater than 3/10 because although both fractions consist of 3 parts, eighths are greater than tenths because when an object is divided into 8 equal parts, each part is larger than when the same object is divided into 10 equal parts.

Comparing fractions that have the same denominator

If two fractions have the same denominator, then the fractions have parts of the same size, and so the fraction with the greater numerator is greater because it has more parts. Once students have this knowledge and understand how to give fractions common denominators, they will be able to compare any two fractions.

Comparing fractions in general

To compare two fractions that do not have the same denominator (or the same numerator), students can first give the fractions a common denominator and then compare those fractions as before. The process of giving fractions a common denominator requires students to find equivalent fractions and is the same process that is used in fraction addition and subtraction, which is discussed later.

Comparing Fractions

Which fraction is greater? Explain how you know.

1. $\dfrac{1}{5}$ or $\dfrac{1}{6}$

2. $\dfrac{2}{5}$ or $\dfrac{2}{7}$

3. $\dfrac{2}{7}$ or $\dfrac{3}{7}$

4. $\dfrac{1}{8}$ or $\dfrac{1}{10}$

Misconceptions in comparing fractions

A common misconception is that such fractions as 4/4 or 5/5 are not equal to each other. Students should understand that these forms are just different ways of writing 1 whole. In contrast, students sometimes think that such fractions as 5/6 and 7/8 *are* equal to each other because both are "one piece away from a whole." Again, by thinking about the common underlying whole for each of these fractions and using their knowledge that 1/6 > 1/8, students will realize that even though the fractions are both 1 piece away from the whole, the size of the pieces is different and that 5/6 < 7/8.

Using benchmarks to compare fractions

Sometimes we can more easily compare fractions by considering how they relate to such benchmark numbers as 1/2 or 1 instead of by using the general methods of using common numerators or common denominators described above. By thinking about how fractions relate to such benchmarks as 1/2 and 1, students can also develop their sense of fractions as numbers. This approach works for only a limited number of examples, however.

Equivalent fractions

When students work with fraction bars and number lines, they should be encouraged to notice that the same fractional amount can be expressed in different ways. Fractions that represent the same number are called *equivalent fractions*. The term "equivalent fractions" is traditional, although we could just as well say "equal fractions" because such fractions represent the same number. To see why multiplying the numerator and denominator of a fraction by the same number results in an equivalent (or equal) fraction, students can subdivide fraction strips as in figure 3.5, or they can subdivide segments on number lines. Students should not just match fractional amounts and count up the number of parts. Rather, they should understand that splitting each part into a number of equal parts causes both the numerator and denominator to be multiplied by that number, as described in figure 3.5. Even though the parts have been split, the same amount of the bar is shaded, it is just divided into a different number of pieces. Since the same amount of the bar is shaded in each instance, all the fractions in figure 3.5 stand for the same number.

Comparing Fractions by Using Benchmarks

Some fractions can be compared by considering how they are related to benchmark

fractions, such as $\frac{1}{2}$ and 1.

1. Which is more, $\frac{3}{5}$ of a sub or $\frac{1}{2}$ of a sub of the same size? Why?

2. Which is more, $\frac{3}{8}$ of a pizza or $\frac{1}{2}$ of a pizza of the same size? Why?

3. Which is more $\frac{7}{8}$ of a bottle of juice or $\frac{8}{8}$ of a bottle of juice of the same size? Why?

4. Which is more, $\frac{5}{6}$ of a pizza or $\frac{7}{8}$ of a pizza of the same size?

Students may find it confusing that we physically *divide* the parts of the fraction bar in figure 3.5, yet numerically we *multiply* the numerator and denominator of 2/3. Help students by asking how the number of parts and the size of the parts are related. Discuss that because the whole amount is not changing, having smaller parts means more of them are needed to make the whole. So the *number* of parts is multiplied to make more parts (and the fraction looks larger with those larger numbers 8/12 in it), but the *size* of the parts (reflected in the unit fraction) becomes smaller, so the size of the fraction really does not change.

By reversing the process and joining pieces, as in figure 3.6, students can also see why dividing the numerator and denominator of a fraction by the same number results in an equivalent fraction. The same amount of the bar is shaded either way, but this amount is described in terms of a different number of parts. This process is called *simplifying* because the denominator becomes smaller (and the unit fraction becomes larger). School books and tests often place too much emphasis on always simplifying answers. Although students should understand simplification and be able to simplify, doing so can interfere with seeing certain patterns, such as when adding and subtracting (e.g., that the product of the denominators can always be used as a common denominator when adding and subtracting).

Note that from a more advanced perspective, we can use multiplication or division by 1 in the form of

$$\frac{n}{n} \left(\text{i.e.,} \frac{2}{2}, \frac{3}{3}, \frac{4}{4}, \text{etc.}\right)$$

to explain why we can multiply or divide the numerator and denominator of a fraction by the same number and produce a fraction that is equal to the original fraction. For example, to show that 2/3 is equal to 8/12 we can multiply by 1 in the form of

$$\frac{4}{4}:$$

$$\frac{2}{3} = \frac{2}{3} \cdot 1 = \frac{2}{3} \cdot \frac{4}{4} = \frac{2 \cdot 4}{3 \cdot 4} = \frac{8}{12}.$$

Since students study equivalent fractions before they learn fraction multiplication, this line of reasoning cannot be used initially. Students need to reason as seen in figures 3.5 and 3.6. When multiplying of fractions has been completed, equivalent fractions can be briefly revisited to discuss how the processes shown pictorially in figures 3.5 and 3.6 can be done numerically by multiplying by some form of 1 = *n/n*.

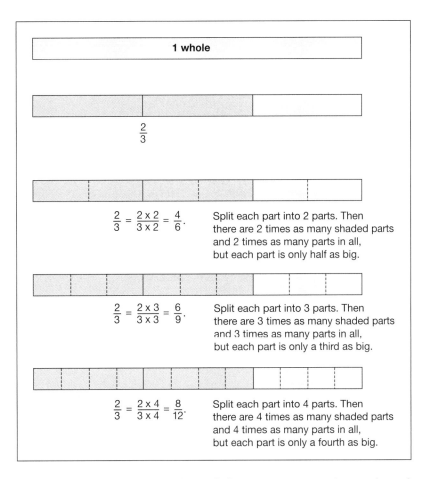

Fig. 3.5. Forming equivalent fractions by splitting parts causes the total number of parts and the number of shaded parts to be multiplied.

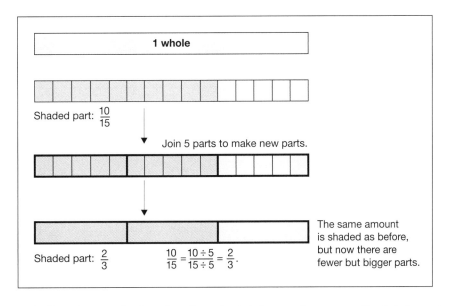

Fig. 3.6. Forming equivalent fractions by joining parts causes the total number of parts and the number of shaded parts to be divided.

Equivalent Fractions in the Multiplication Table

x	1	2	3	4	5	6	7	8	9	10
1	1	2	3	4	5	6	7	8	9	10
2	2	4	6	8	10	12	14	16	18	20
3	3	6	9	12	15	18	21	24	27	30
4	4	8	12	16	20	24	28	32	36	40
5	5	10	15	20	25	30	35	40	45	50
6	6	12	18	24	30	36	42	48	54	60
7	7	14	21	28	35	42	49	56	63	70
8	8	16	24	32	40	48	57	64	72	80
9	9	18	27	36	45	54	63	72	81	90
10	10	20	30	40	50	60	70	80	90	100

You can use the multiplication table to find equivalent fractions.

$$\overset{\times 2}{\frac{2}{5}} = \frac{4}{10} \qquad \overset{\times 3}{\frac{2}{5}} = \frac{6}{15} \qquad \overset{\times 4}{\frac{2}{5}} = \frac{8}{20} \qquad \overset{\times 5}{\frac{2}{5}} = \frac{10}{25} \qquad \overset{\times 6}{\frac{2}{5}} = \frac{12}{30}$$

$$\underset{\times 2}{\quad} \qquad \underset{\times 3}{\quad} \qquad \underset{\times 4}{\quad} \qquad \underset{\times 5}{\quad} \qquad \underset{\times 6}{\quad}$$

1. Use the multiplication table to find four more fractions that are equivalent to $\frac{2}{5}$.

2. Color rows 3 and 7 in the table. Use the table to find nine equivalent fractions for $\frac{3}{7} = $.

$$\frac{3}{7} = \qquad \frac{3}{7} = \qquad \frac{3}{7} = \qquad \frac{3}{7} = \qquad \frac{3}{7} = \qquad \frac{3}{7} = \qquad \frac{3}{7} = \qquad \frac{3}{7} = \qquad \frac{3}{7}$$

Make Equivalent Fractions

Fill in the blanks to make equivalent fractions. Show what number you multiplied or divided the numerator and denominator by.

$$\frac{4}{5} = \frac{8}{} \qquad \frac{6}{8} = \frac{}{4} \qquad \frac{3}{8} = \frac{15}{} \qquad \frac{3}{4} = \frac{}{24} \qquad \frac{8}{12} = \frac{2}{}$$

Adding and subtracting fractions

Fraction addition and subtraction is a focus in grade 5. An important special case is that of adding and subtracting fractions that have the same denominator.

Adding and subtracting fractions with like denominators

Students should understand that when they are adding or subtracting fractions that have the same denominator, they are working with like parts, so the answer is the fraction that tells them how many parts are in the result. Such supports as the drawings in figure 3.7 can help students understand why the numerators are added or subtracted but the denominators remain the same when adding or subtracting fractions that have the same denominator.

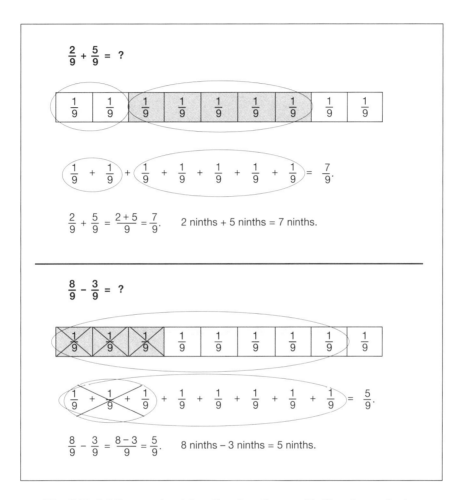

Fig. 3.7. Adding and subtracting fractions with like denominators

Adding and subtracting fractions with different denominators

The general case of adding or subtracting fractions reduces to the special case of adding or subtracting fractions that have the same denominator by finding equivalent fractions that have the same denominator.

If two fractions do not have the same denominator, then they are not expressed in terms of like parts. When students give the fractions a common denominator, they express both fractions in terms of like parts so that the number of parts can be added or subtracted. For example, when 1/2 cup of orange juice is mixed with 1/3 cup of grapefruit juice, how much juice is in the mixture? Halves and thirds are not like parts, so we need a part of a common size to express the total amount of juice as a fraction. See figure 3.8a. Because 1/2 = 3/6 and 1/3 = 2/6, both fractions can be expressed in terms of sixths. The problem of adding 1 half and 1 third is reduced to the problem of adding 3 sixths and 2 sixths, which is 5 sixths. Expressed symbolically, 1/2 + 1/3 = 3/6 + 2/6 = 5/6, so the mixture contains 5/6 of a cup of juice.

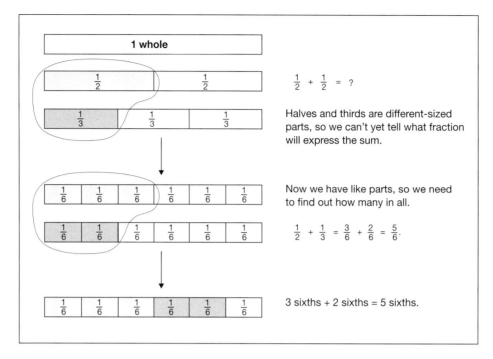

Fig. 3.8a. To add fractions with different denominators, find a common denominator to make like parts.

Finding common denominators

How can students find common denominators for adding or subtracting (as well as for comparing) fractions? *Any* common denominator can be used to add or subtract fractions; it does not have to be the least common denominator. One common denominator that always works is the product of the two denominators, although the result can be a larger number than is desirable to work with.

To find a common denominator, a good first step is for students to check whether one denominator is a multiple of the other. If so, then only one fraction needs to be changed into an equivalent one to give the two fractions a common denominator. For example, to give 3/5 and 8/15 common denominators, only 3/5 needs to be changed into an equivalent fraction, namely, into 9/15 (by multiplying both the numerator and denominator by 3).

If neither denominator is a multiple of the other, then both fractions must be changed into equivalent ones to give them common denominators. For example, one common denominator for 3/8 and 1/6 is the product of the denominators, 8 × 6, or 48. Alternatively, students can make a list of multiples of one of the denominators (working with the larger denominator is more efficient) and look for a number in the list that is also a multiple of the other denominator. For example, to give 3/8 and 1/6 common denominators, students can list the multiples of 8 until they find a multiple of 6: listing 8, 16, 24, … and stopping when they recognize 24 as a multiple of 6. Often students can simply think of a number that is a multiple of both denominators and do not have to use any list process at all. Once a common denominator is found, students can write both fractions as equivalent fractions with that denominator and proceed as in the previous example for adding or subtracting fractions that have the same denominator.

The process of finding common denominators to compare fractions is the very same process that was just described for finding common denominators to add or subtract fractions. Students can then use what they know about comparing fractions with the same denominators: the fraction with the larger numerator is more because it has more of the unit fractions.

What Common Denominator Is Good to Use?

The fraction problems in each group have something in common.

Group 1	Group 2	Group 3

$$\frac{7}{16} - \frac{3}{8} =$$ $$\frac{7}{10} - \frac{1}{3} =$$ $$\frac{7}{8} - \frac{1}{12} =$$

$$\frac{2}{3} + \frac{2}{21} =$$ $$\frac{2}{5} + \frac{3}{4} =$$ $$\frac{3}{4} - \frac{1}{6} =$$

$$\frac{13}{24} - \frac{1}{3} =$$ $$\frac{3}{7} + \frac{1}{9} =$$ $$\frac{5}{9} + \frac{5}{6} =$$

How did you find a common denominator for the problems in group 1?

How did you find a common denominator for the problems in group 2?

How did you find a common denominator for the problems in group 3?

Make another problem for group 1.

Make another problem for group 2.

Make another problem for group 3.

(Note that although students may have used the same method to find a common denominator for the problems in groups 2 and 3, for the problems in group 2, the least common denominator that can be used is the product of the two denominators. But for the problems in group 3, a smaller denominator than the product is possible. Students can often generate a smaller denominator just by thinking or by saying multiples of the larger denominator and seeing whether the smaller denominator divides a multiple. Such a multiple will be a common denominator.) These groups demonstrate that different methods are effective for different problems, as discussed above. Also, finding the least common denominator is just one of the easy methods for groups 1 and 2 and is not really necessary for group 3.

Adding and subtracting mixed numbers

Mixed numbers often arise in situations that involve measurements. For example, a recipe might call for $3\frac{1}{2}$ cups of flour, or an amount of rainfall might be described as $1\frac{3}{8}$ inches. To add and subtract mixed numbers, students must be able to coordinate whole-number addition and subtraction with fraction addition and subtraction and to regroup appropriately between fractions and whole numbers. Alternatively, mixed-number addition and subtraction can be carried out by first converting the mixed numbers to improper fractions.

Fraction Problem Solving

1. Sean spent $\frac{2}{5}$ of his money on a computer game that cost $18. How much money did Sean have at first, before he bought the computer game?

   Note that students could reason about a fraction-bar drawing to solve this problem, as in Susan's solution, shown below.

   Susan's solution: I drew all of Sean's money as my whole. Then I divided it into 5 equal parts.

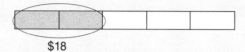

   $18

   I knew that 2 of the parts are $18, so each part is $9. So all 5 parts are 5 times $9, which is $45.

   Similar fraction-bar drawings can help students solve the next problems as well.

2. Amanda used $\frac{2}{5}$ of a liter of paint. Taryn used $\frac{1}{10}$ of a liter less paint than Amanda. How much paint did Taryn use? How much paint did the two girls use altogether?

   (Solution: Taryn used $\frac{4}{10} - \frac{1}{10} = \frac{3}{10}$ of a liter, and altogether, the girls used $\frac{4}{10} + \frac{3}{10} = \frac{7}{10}$ of a liter of paint.)

3. Carlton had $72. Then he spent $\frac{1}{4}$ of his money on books and $\frac{3}{8}$ of his money on sports equipment. How much money did Carlton have left?
   (Answer: Carlton had $27 left. Students could first draw a bar divided into fourths, then subdivide into eighths to help them solve this problem.)

4. We ate $\frac{5}{12}$ of a watermelon at lunch. At supper we ate $\frac{1}{4}$ of the watermelon. How much of the watermelon do we still have to eat?
   (Answer: We have eaten $\frac{5}{12} + \frac{3}{12} = \frac{7}{12}$ of a watermelon, so we have $\frac{5}{12}$ still to eat.)

5. Sauline lives $\frac{5}{8}$ miles from his grandmother's house and $\frac{3}{5}$ of a mile from his uncle's house. Who lives closer to Sauline? How much closer? (Answer: I need to change these fractions both to 40ths: $\frac{25}{40}$ and $\frac{24}{40}$. Sauline's uncle lives closer to Sauline's house than his grandmother does, $\frac{1}{40}$ of a mile closer.

Fraction Problem Solving—*Continued*

6. After a store sold $\frac{4}{9}$ of its sale DVDs, there were 35 sale DVDs left. How many sale DVDs did the store have at first?

(Note: To solve this problem, students could draw a bar divided into ninths. Five of the ninths are left, and this amount is 35 DVDs, so each ninth is 7 DVDs and the total was 63 DVDs.)

Converting between mixed numbers and improper fractions

A mixed number consists of a whole-number part and a fractional part, and stands for the sum of those two parts. For example, $4^2/_3$ stands for 4 + 2/3. Mixed numbers can also be written as improper fractions. To convert a mixed number to an improper fraction, students can view the mixed number as a sum. Figure 3.8 shows a type of picture students can use to help them begin to understand how to convert mixed numbers to improper fractions.

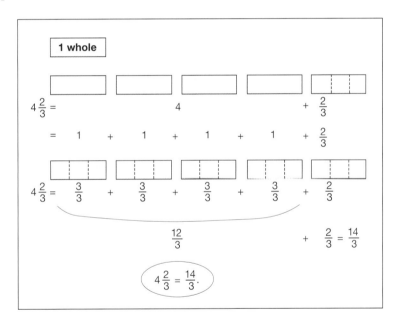

Fig. 3.8b. Developing a method for converting mixed numbers to improper fractions

Methods for adding and subtracting mixed numbers

To add or subtract mixed numbers, students can work separately with the fractional parts and the whole-number parts. However, students must take care to regroup appropriately if necessary. Figure 3.8c indicates some ways students might reason about a mixed-number subtraction problem.

Another way to add or subtract mixed numbers is to convert the mixed numbers to improper fractions and then to add or subtract the improper fractions. Generally, the result should then be converted back to a mixed number.

Mixed Numbers and Improper Fractions

Materials: Each student needs 7 identical fifths-strips. These are strips of paper or cardstock, with "1 whole" on one side and subdivided into 5 fifths on the other, as shown. Students fold the strips along the dashed lines so that they can show between 1 fifth and 5 fifths.

One side:

1 whole

The other side:

$\frac{1}{5}$	$\frac{1}{5}$	$\frac{1}{5}$	$\frac{1}{5}$	$\frac{1}{5}$

Write these numbers on the board:

$$3\frac{2}{5} \quad 5\frac{4}{5} \quad 6\frac{1}{5} \quad 2\frac{3}{5}$$

Discuss with students how to make these mixed numbers with their fraction strips. Ask them: How do you know how many 1 whole strips to use to make the mixed number? How do you know how many more 1/5 pieces are needed?

Have students build each mixed number with their strips. Then ask the students to predict how many fifths each number is and to check their predictions by turning over the strips and counting the fifths. Ask students to write the mixed numbers as improper fractions. This activity can lead into a discussion of more efficient methods for converting mixed numbers to improper fractions.

Problem solving with fractions

The problem examples for mixed numbers on page 48 and for the earlier addition and subtraction of fractions on pages 44 and 45 exemplify several aspects of problem-solving opportunities that are valuable for students. First, the problems are mixed in terms of the operation required. Therefore, students must read the problem and try to understand the situation. They can make a drawing of the situation to help them. We have shown such drawings in the text and for some problem examples. Some problems are so simple in structure that students do not need a drawing but can move directly to a written computation. For example, in the mixed-number problem 3, many students will just write the three numbers vertically and add them. Others may just add those numbers mentally because the numbers are easy (¾ plus ¾ makes 1½, plus the other ½ makes 2, plus 2 is 4, plus 2 from the 1 and 1 makes 6).

Second, the unknown number in these problems is not always the result of a simple addition or subtraction. The unknown might be an unknown addend, such as in the mixed-number problem 1 on page 48. This problem might be represented by an equation showing this unknown-addend situation as 1¾ + ? = 3¼. The student then reflects on this equation to decide on a solution method. One student might add on from 1¾ up to 3¼: 1¾ up to 2 is ¼, and 1¼ more up to the total 3¼ makes 1²⁄₄, which is 1½. Another might write a vertical subtraction problem. Students solving comparison problems such as the mixed-

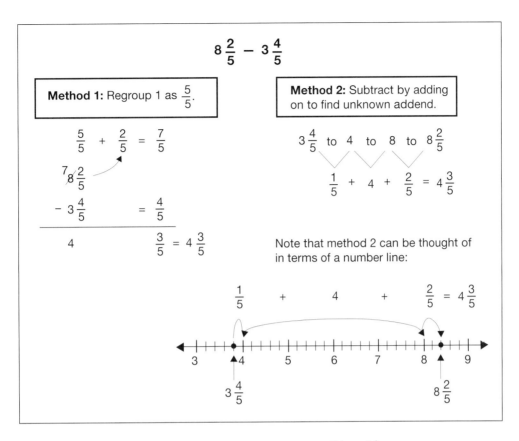

Fig. 3.8c. Methods for solving $8^2/_5 - 3^4/_5$

number problem 2 also vary in their solutions. Some add on up to the total, and others write a subtraction problem.

Third, several two-step problems are included. Students in grades 3, 4, and 5 should be solving problems with two or more steps. These problems generate interesting discussions because many such problems can be solved in more than one way. For example, in the final mixed-number problem involving a perimeter of a rectangle, the total and one side are known (page 48). Some students may double that side $(8\frac{1}{4} + 8\frac{1}{4} = 16\frac{2}{4})$, subtract those two sides from the total 28 $(28 - 16\frac{2}{4} = 11\frac{2}{4})$, and then find what two equal sides make $11\frac{2}{4}$ (for example, splitting $10\frac{2}{4}$ into two equal parts makes $5\frac{1}{4}$ and then splitting the remaining 1 into two halves adds $\frac{1}{2}$ to each $5\frac{1}{4}$, so $5\frac{3}{4}$). However, some students will know that two adjacent sides of a rectangle make half the total perimeter. Thus $8\frac{1}{4} + ? = 14$, so the next side will be $5\frac{3}{4}$ (adding on is easy here). This method is much easier. The first part of the first method also demonstrates that not simplifying an answer can help: The $\frac{2}{4}$ in $10\frac{2}{4}$ was ready to separate into $\frac{1}{4}$ and $\frac{1}{4}$; simplifying $\frac{2}{4}$ in $\frac{1}{2}$ would have required unsimplifying it again to find the two equal parts.

Finally, an important part of problem solving is asking as one solves and at the end, "Does my answer make sense?" The answer is not a simple issue of always rounding or estimating, although these tactics can be helpful. In the first mixed-number problem, one can easily put the answer into the situation and check by adding mentally (or in written form): $1\frac{3}{4} + 1\frac{1}{2}$ is 2 and 1 and 1/4, which is $3\frac{1}{4}$. In problem 2 the solver can see that $8\frac{3}{4}$ plus 1 equals $9\frac{3}{4}$, which is more than $9\frac{5}{8}$, so the answer $\frac{7}{8}$ is roughly correct. But these fractions are so simple that it is easier just to check by adding on: $8\frac{3}{4}$ up to 9 is $\frac{1}{4}$, which is $\frac{2}{8}$, plus the $\frac{5}{8}$ in $9\frac{5}{8}$, so $\frac{7}{8}$.

The problem-solving processes discussed for these problem sets are really informal algebraic problem solving: Students focus on understanding the problem situation and then representing it with an equation,

---

Mixed Number Addition and Subtraction

1. At first there were $1\frac{3}{4}$ pounds of apples in a bag. After adding some more apples, there were $3\frac{1}{4}$ pounds of apples in the bag. How many pounds of apples were added to the bag?

   (Answer: $1\frac{2}{4} = 1\frac{1}{2}$ pounds.)

2. One shelf is $9\frac{5}{8}$ inches wide. Another shelf is $8\frac{3}{4}$ inches wide. How much wider is the first shelf?

   (Answer: $\frac{7}{8}$ inches)

3. A recipe for punch calls for $2\frac{3}{4}$ cups of grape juice, $1\frac{3}{4}$ cups of apple juice, and $1\frac{1}{2}$ cups of seltzer water. How many cups of punch will the recipe make?
   (Answer: 6 cups)

4. Melanie is making a rectangular fence for her rabbit. She has 28 feet of fencing. She makes the first side $8\frac{1}{4}$ feet long. How long will the next side be?

   (Answer: See discussion in the next section: $5\frac{3}{4}$.)

---

a drawing, or calculations. The problems here are simple enough that students do not need the formal algebraic language or formal methods of solving equations. But experience with all types of problems, including multistep problems that can eventually be represented in equations and problems complex enough to require the help of a drawing, fosters informal understandings that can make later algebraic methods more comprehensible to students. Such problems are solved by students in other countries, so students in the United States should also have an opportunity for such problem solving at these grades.

Using money and clocks to develop fraction sense for some fractions

Some teachers have found that suitable mental addition and subtraction problems done with the aid of thinking about money or about an analog clock can help students develop their sense of fraction addition and subtraction.

Fourths, halves, tenths, twentieths, and hundredths lend themselves to thinking about money, because a quarter (25 cents) is 1/4 of a dollar, 50 cents is 1/2 of a dollar, a dime (10 cents) is 1/10 of a dollar, a nickel (5 cents) is 1/20 of a dollar, and a penny (1 cent) is 1/100 of a dollar. So to add 1/2 + 1/4 mentally, students might think of the sum as 3 quarters, which is 3/4 of a dollar. Similarly, to calculate

$$1\frac{1}{10} - \frac{1}{2},$$

students might think of the problem as 1 dollar and a dime minus 50 cents, which leaves 6 dimes, or 6/10 of a dollar, remaining. Viewing the 6 dimes as 3 groups of 20 cents, and viewing each 20 cents as 1/5 of a dollar, students can see that 6/10 can also be expressed as 3/5. Thinking about such monetary equivalents can also help with connecting certain fractions and decimals, which is a focus in grade 4.

Halves, thirds, fourths, sixths, and twelfths lend themselves to thinking about clocks, because 1/2 of an hour (30 minutes), 1/3 of an hour (20 minutes), 1/4 of an hour (15 minutes), 1/6 of an hour (10 minutes), and 1/12 of an hour (5 minutes) are not too hard to picture on an analog clockface. To subtract 1/2 – 1/3 mentally, students might picture going back 20 minutes from half an hour, which leaves 10 minutes, or 1/6 of an hour, remaining. To add 1/2 + 1/3 mentally, students might view the sum as half an hour plus another 20 minutes, which is 50 minutes, or 5 sets of 10 minutes, or 5/6 of an hour.

Important for both of these applications is not just getting answers but understanding fractions. And students do need to go beyond these situations to develop general methods for adding and subtracting fractions.

Mental Addition and Subtraction Problems

Money problems

$$\frac{3}{4}+\frac{3}{4} \qquad 3\frac{1}{4}-\frac{1}{2} \qquad \frac{1}{10}+\frac{1}{4}$$

$$\frac{1}{4}+\frac{1}{20} \qquad 4\frac{1}{2}+2\frac{3}{4} \qquad 5-\frac{7}{10}$$

Clock problems

$$\frac{3}{4}-\frac{1}{2} \qquad \frac{1}{6}+\frac{1}{6} \qquad \frac{1}{12}+\frac{1}{2}+\frac{1}{12}$$

$$\frac{1}{2}+\frac{1}{6} \qquad \frac{2}{3}+\frac{1}{12} \qquad \frac{3}{4}-\frac{1}{12}$$

Fractions and division

When one submarine sandwich is divided equally among 5 people, each person's share is 1/5 of the sub. What if 2 identical subs are shared equally among 5 people? On the one hand, we can say that each person's share is 2 ÷ 5, but another way to describe this amount is as 2/5 of a sub. Figure 3.9 shows why this is so. Similarly, if 3 identical subs are shared equally among 5 people, each person's share can be described both as 3 ÷ 5 and as 3/5 of a sub (see fig. 3.9 again). In general, when *A* things are divided equally among *B* shares, each share receives *A/B* of a thing. Therefore in general,

$$A \div B = \frac{A}{B},$$

and this equation describes a primary link between division and fractions. This connection is the reason we can use fraction notation to show division. But whether

$$\frac{A}{B}$$

means division or a fraction can be confusing to students. So

$$3 \div 5 = \frac{3}{5}$$

could be read as "3 divided by 5 is the fraction three-fifths."

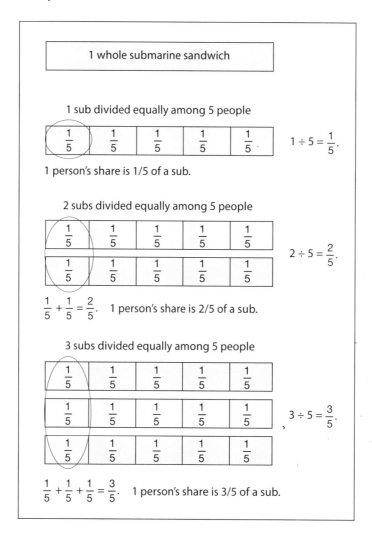

Fig. 3.9. Showing why *A* things divided equally among *B* shares results in *A/B* things in each share, or in other words, showing why *A* ÷ *B* = *A/B*

The connection between fractions and division is especially important when students convert fractions to decimals by dividing the numerator by the denominator and continue the division into decimal places in later grades.

Dividing Submarine Sandwiches

A fifth-grade class traveled to a field trip in four separate cars. The school provided a lunch of submarine sandwiches (all of the same size) for each group. When they stopped for lunch, the subs were cut and shared as follows:

- The first group had four people and shared three subs equally.

- The second group had five people and shared four subs equally.

- The third group had eight people and shared seven subs equally.

- The last group had five people and shared three subs equally.

When they returned from the field trip, the students began to argue that the distribution of sandwiches had not been fair, that some students got more to eat. Were they right? Or did everyone get the same amount? How much of a sub did each person get, assuming that the pieces were cut equally?

Decimals

In fourth grade, students develop an understanding of decimals, including the connection between fractions and decimals. Students come to understand that our notation for decimals is an extension of the base-ten system that we use for whole numbers. The structure of the base-ten place-value system—which allows 1-for-10 trades—extends to the right of the decimal point. This section looks into some of the important decimal ideas that underlie learning about adding and subtracting decimals, which is a focus in grade 5.

Decimals extend the base-ten system for writing whole numbers

The decimal system is extremely powerful because its essential structure extends nicely to nonwhole numbers. If students attend to place value and to the relationship between the values of adjacent places, then the reasoning they use to add, subtract, and compare whole numbers extends directly to decimals.

The structure of the decimal system

The base-ten system for writing whole numbers relies on place value. We use the ten *digits* 0, 1, 2, 3, 4, 5, 6, 7, 8, 9 to write numbers as strings of digits. But the value that a digit represents depends on the position the digit is in. Starting at the ones place, the value of each place to the left is ten times the value of the place to its right, as indicated in figure 3.10. So we can think of each place's value as obtained by "bundling up" ten of the units of the place to the right to form a new unit. When we represent a number with a string of digits, each digit stands for that many of its place's value and the number as a whole stands for the combined value. So 1234 stands for the combined amount formed by 1 thousand, 2 hundreds, 3 tens, and 4 ones.

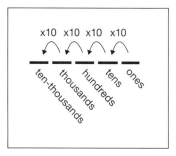

**Fig. 3.10. The value of each place is ten times
the value of the place to its right.**

To extend the decimal system to decimals, we have to extend the key structure of the decimal system—that the value of each place is ten times the value of the place to its right. As figure 3.10 shows, moving to the left across the places, the values of the places are multiplied by 10. So moving to the *right* across the places, the values of the places are *divided by 10,* as indicated in figure 3.11. Viewing the values of the places in this way allows us to extend the decimal system to places to the right of the ones place.

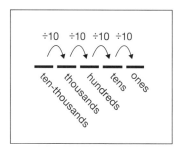

**Fig. 3.11. Moving to the right, the value of
each place is divided by 10.**

To extend the decimal system to include numbers that have digits to the right of the ones place, we continue the pattern of dividing a unit at a given place by 10 to make the next unit to the right. See figure 3.12. At the ones place, dividing the unit 1 into ten equal pieces creates a new unit, a tenth. We can record between 0 and 9 tenths in the tenths place to the right of the ones place, and a digit in the tenths place represents that many tenths. A tenth is the fraction 1/10, but we write it as 0.1 or just .1 in decimal notation. In the tenths place, dividing a tenth into ten equal pieces creates a new unit, a hundredth. We can record between 0 and 9 hundredths in the hundredths place to the right of the tenths place, and a digit in the hundredths place represents that many hundredths. The process of dividing a unit at a given place by 10 to create a new, smaller unit that is recorded in the place to the right continues indefinitely.

Just as 123 stands for the combined amount made from 1 hundred, 2 tens, and 3 ones, so too 1.23 stands for the combined amount made from 1 one, 2 tenths, and 3 hundredths. In terms of money, 1.23 can be thought of as the amount made by 1 dollar, 2 dimes (tenths of a dollar), and 3 cents (hundredths of a dollar). As lengths, 1.2 can be formed by placing lengths of 1 unit and 2 tenths of a unit end-to-end, and 1.23 can be formed by placing lengths of 1 unit, 2 tenths of a unit, and 3 hundredths of a unit end-to-end, as in figure 3.13. Decimal lengths can be nicely connected with the metric system by using 1 meter as a unit of length. One tenth of a meter is a decimeter, one hundredth of a meter is a centimeter, and one thousandth of a meter is a millimeter. To get a feel for decimals down to the thousandths place, students can make and measure decimal lengths using a meter as a unit of length, as shown in figure 3.5.

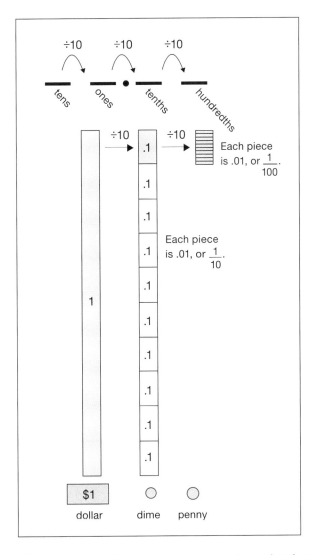

**Fig. 3.12. The decimal system extends to numbers that have digits
to the right of the ones place.**

This page is too small to show millimeters as tenths of centimeters, but this relationship can be seen by students with real centimeters and millimeters.

Symmetry in the values of decimal places

Note the symmetry in the values of the places in decimals: the symmetry is around the ones place, as shown in figure 3.14, not around the decimal point. Students sometimes mistakenly think that a decimal number should have a "oneths place" because they expect symmetry around the decimal point. Some students do not recognize the distinction between symmetrically related places. For example, they may not distinguish between tens and tenths, hundreds and hundredths, thousands and thousandths, and so on, because of the subtle differences in pronunciation. Teachers must take care to pronounce the place-value terms clearly and to draw students' attention to the distinction between the values of places to the left and right of the decimal point.

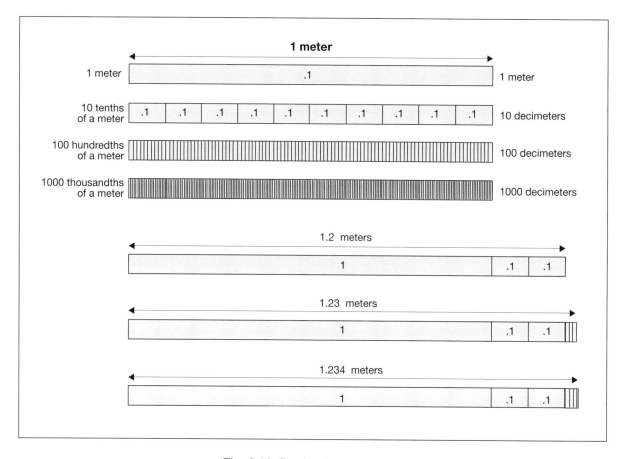

Fig. 3.13. Decimals as lengths

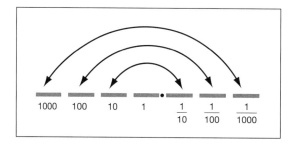

Fig. 3.14. The symmetry in values of decimal places around the ones place

Writing and saying decimals

When comparing, adding, or subtracting decimals, students are often helped by rewriting a decimal to express explicitly the zero value of one or more places to the right of the rightmost nonzero value in the decimal. For example, the following decimal representations all stand for the same number:

0.23,
0.230,
0.2300,
0.23000,
0.230000,

and so on. We can append as many zeros as we want to the right of 0.23, and the result will still represent the same number because we are simply saying explicitly that there are 0 thousandths, 0 ten-thousandths, 0 hundred-thousandths, and so on, in 0.23.

Commonly, decimals that have nonzero values only below the ones place are written with a 0 in the ones place. For example, we usually write 0.2 instead of just writing .2. This practice is simply a convention that helps us notice the decimal point. To write .2 instead of 0.2 is perfectly correct.

A common practice is to say decimals according to their last nonzero decimal place and to say "and" for the decimal point. For example, we usually say "one and twenty-three hundredths" for 1.23 and "one and two-hundred thirty-four thousandths" for 1.234. Although students should know these cultural conventions for saying decimals, we have no mathematical need for saying decimals this way. From a mathematical perspective, perfectly acceptable expressions for 1.234 are "one point two three four" or "one and two tenths and three hundredths and four thousandths." In fact, we cannot use the usual conventions when we read infinite decimals. For example, the number pi, which is 3.1415 … , should be read as "three point one four one five…." Furthermore, the rationale that underlies why decimals can be said in the conventional way is not immediately evident and involves some reasoning that is discussed in a later section. Learning to say decimals in the conventional way should not be a priority.

Which Decimals Are Equal?

Which of the following decimals are equal to one another, and why?

0.2030	0.2003	0.203	0.0203	.203	0.20300

(Solution: 0.2030 = 0.203 = .203 = 0.20300 because they are all 2 tenths and 3 thousandths, but 0.2003 is 2 tenths and 3 ten-thousandths; and 0.0203 is 2 hundredths and 3 ten-thousandths.)

Comparing and ordering decimals

For students to deepen their understanding of decimals, and in particular for them to understand how to estimate sums and differences involving decimals, students must understand how decimals compare. A foundational understanding is that the decimal places of larger value "count more." But the tricky part of this concept is the direction in which decimal places "count more." Students are used to whole numbers that get larger as you move to places to the left. With decimals, this outcome is still true, but the reversal of the names and their whole-number meanings makes some students think that places are getting larger as you move to the right (these students think hundredths are larger than tenths because hundreds are larger than tens).

Comparing like places, starting at the place of greatest value

The decimal system has a uniform structure that goes across the decimal point: the value of each place is ten times the value of the place to its immediate right. Therefore, comparing decimals is just like comparing whole numbers. In either instance we *compare like places, starting at the place of highest value.* We can compare numbers this way because in the decimal system, given any decimal place, its value is greater than any (finite) decimal number that can be made using only places of lower value. For example a hundred is greater than any number that can be made using only tens and ones. Ten is greater than any number that can be made using only ones, tenths, and hundredths (and other lower places). A tenth is greater than any number that can be made using only hundredths and thousandths (and other lower places).

Because the value of a given decimal place "counts more" than the values that can be made from lower places, the key to comparing either whole numbers or decimals is to compare digits in like places, starting at the place of highest value in which a nonzero digit appears. For example, to compare 0.12 and 0.099, a helpful tactic is to align like places in the numbers first:

0.12

0.099

The place of highest value in which a nonzero digit appears is the tenths place. Accordingly, 0.12 is greater than 0.099 because 0.12 has a 1 in the tenths place but 0.099 has a 0 in the tenths place. Even though 0.099 has several large digits in places below the tenths place, the combined value still does not exceed the value of the tenths place, in the same way that even though 99 has large digits below the hundreds place, their combined value still does not exceed the value of the hundreds place.

To more easily align places of the same value when comparing decimals, students can append zeros and work with decimals with the same number of places. For example, to compare 0.12 and 0.099, students are helped by rewriting 0.12 as 0.120 and aligning like places:

0.120

0.099

Misconceptions in comparing decimals

Misconceptions that students have about decimals often surface when they compare decimals. A common misconception is for students to treat the portion to the right of the decimal point as if it were a whole number, thus leading them to decide incorrectly, for example, that 0.099 is greater than 0.12 because 99 is greater than 12 or that 3.199 is greater than 3.21 because 199 is greater than 21. Some of these students may view 3.199 incorrectly as 3 and 199 tenths and 3.21 incorrectly as 3 and 21 tenths (Steinle, Stacey, and Chambers 2002; Stacey 2005). However, these students may understand numbers such as 1.4 and 1.05 correctly as 1 and 4 tenths and 1 and 5 hundredths and compare these numbers correctly.

Students can also have other misconceptions about decimal comparison (Stacey, Helme, and Steinle 2001). For example, some students believe that any number that has thousandths must be smaller than any number that has hundredths because thousandths are smaller than hundreds. For example, these students might believe incorrectly that 6.321 is smaller than 6.19 because 6.321 has entries in the thousandths place but 6.19 has entries only down to the hundredths place. Other students may confuse decimals with fractions or even with negative numbers, viewing 0.3 as 1/3 or as something like −3. Some of these students may think, incorrectly, that 0.3 is greater than 0.4 because 1/3 is greater than 1/4. Others may come to the same incorrect conclusion because −3 is greater than −4. Because of the many subtle misconceptions that students can develop, they should have experience with comparing a variety of pairs of decimals and should repeatedly think of meanings of money or look at metric lengths or make the decimals have the same number of places so that they have the opportunity to confront these and other misconceptions.

Compare Decimals

For each pair of decimals, circle the number that is GREATER or circle both numbers if they are equal.

(1) 0.3 0.04

(2) 3.3 3.25

(3) 0.2 0.20

(4) 0.2 0.02

(5) 2.03 2.004

(6) 1.125 1.6

(7) 8.451 8.2

(8) 16.21 16.212

(9) 0.07 0.2

(10) 8.7 8.777

(11) 12.3 12.1234

(12) 0.0067 0.0670

(Answers: (1) 0.3 = 0.30; (2) 3.3 = 3.30; (3) = ; (4) 0.2 = 0.20; (5) 2.03 = 2.030; (6) 1.6 = 1.600; (7) 8.451; (8) 16.212; (9) 0.2 = 0.20; (10) 8.777; (11) 12.3; (12) 0.0670)

Decimals on number lines

One way to think about decimals is as "filling in" a number line in successive stages. Initially, whole numbers are plotted on the number line, then numbers with tenths are plotted in between the whole numbers, then numbers with hundredths are plotted in between the tenths, then numbers with thousandths are plotted in between the hundredths, and so on. For example, as indicated in figure 3.15, between 6 and 7 appear the tenths 6.1, 6.2, 6.3, 6.4, 6.5, 6.6, 6.7, 6.8, 6.9. Then between each of these numbers appear hundredths. For example, between 6.3 and 6.4 appear the hundredths 6.31, 6.32, 6.33, ... , 6.37, 6.38, 6.39. Between each of these numbers appear thousandths. For example, between 6.32 and 6.33 appear the thousandths 6.321, 6.322, 6.323, 6.324, ... 6.328, 6.329. Between each adjacent pair of thousandths appear ten-thousandths, between each pair of ten-thousandths appear hundred-thousandths, and so on. This same process of filling in each larger place by ten of the smaller place is also shown in figure 3.13 with metric lengths. Figure 3.15 shows how the process of zooming in can continue on and on.

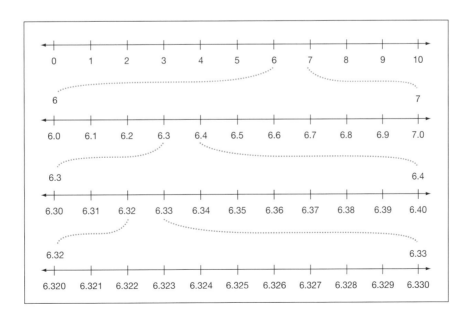

Fig. 3.15. Zooming in on portions of a number line to see tenths, hundredths, and thousandths

Decimals on Number Lines

Write the decimals that the points on the number lines below represent.

A =   B =   C =   D =

E =   F =   G =   H =

(Answers: A = 5.71; B = 5.77; C = 5.83; D = 5.89; E = 8.422; F = 8.426; G = 8.434; H = 8.439. Some students are helped by writing a zero after each of the endpoints before they begin, so that 5.7, 5.8, and 5.9 become 5.70, 5.80, and 5.90 and so that 8.42, 8.43, and 8.44 become 8.420, 8.430, and 8.440.)

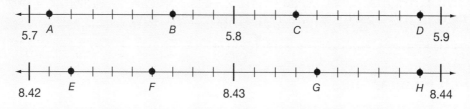

Decimals between Decimals on Number Lines

1. Locate and label a decimal between 0.4 and 0.5 on the number line below.

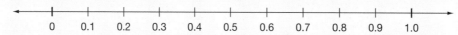

2. Locate and label two decimals between 2.1 and 2.2 on the number line below.

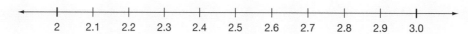

3. Locate and label two decimals between 0.25 and 0.28 on the number line below.

For the activity above, some students will be helped by adding zeroes to the ends of some of the decimals.

Rounding decimals

To round a decimal to a given place means to find a decimal that is closest to the given decimal and has only zero values in places lower than the given place. For example, 12.345 rounded to the tenths place is 12.3 because 12.3 is the decimal with values only down to the tenths place that 12.345 is closest to. The terminology "round to the nearest tenth" can also be used.

To round a decimal to a given place, students can think about the list of decimals that have nonzero values only down to that place. Students can also think about a number line that has tick marks whose distance apart is the value of the given place. For example, when rounding to the nearest tenth, students should think about the list

0.0, 0.1, 0.2, 0.3, ... , 0.9, 1.0, 1.2, ... , 1.9, 2.0, 2.1, 2.2, ... , 9.9, 10.0, 10.1, ...

(which they may prefer to think of as extending vertically upward instead of to the right) or about a number line labeled in tenths. To round, students must first find the two adjacent numbers in the list or labeled on the number line that the given number is between and then determine which of those two numbers the given number is closest to. The decimal 12.345 is between 12.3 and 12.4, which students can indicate by writing 12.4 above 12.345 and 12.3 below:

12.4	or	12.400
12.345		12.345
12.3	or	12.300

Half way between 12.3 and 12.4 is 12.35. Because of the 4 in the hundredths place of 12.345, it is closer to 12.3 than to 12.4, so we round down to 12.3.

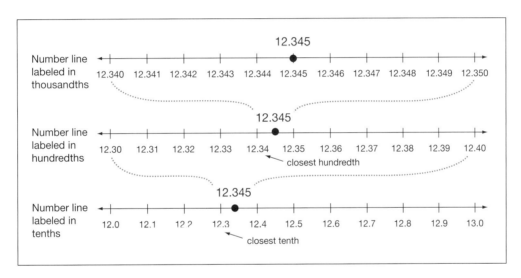

Fig. 3.15a. Rounding 12.345 to the tenths place is like "zooming out" to
a number line labeled in the tenths.

In a sense, rounding a decimal involves "zooming out" to an appropriately labeled number line. For example, the decimal 12.345 might be most naturally viewed as placed on a number line with tick marks labeled in the thousandths, as at the top of figure 3.15a. To round to the nearest tenth, students need to figure out where 12.345 is located on a number line with tick marks labeled in the tenths. Finding this number line labeled in the tenths is really like "zooming out" from a number line labeled in the thousandths to one labeled in the hundredths, and finally to the desired number line, as indicated in figure 3.15a. Using a meter strip marked in millimeters, centimeters, and decimeters (as in figure 3.13) and thinking of labeling lengths as if this were a number line can also be helpful because all the various smaller units are embedded within the larger units.

When rounding, the usual convention is to round ties up. So to round 12.345 to the hundredths place, we round to 12.35 because 12.345 is exactly half way between 12.34 and 12.35 and to break the tie we round up.

Adding and subtracting decimals

To add and subtract decimals, students use the same ideas and methods that they use when they add and subtract whole numbers. Students must understand that only digits in like places can be added or subtracted because digits in like places refer to the same underlying unit amount. For example, when adding 1.2 + 3.45, the 5 in the hundredths place of 3.45 should not be added to the 2 in the tenths place of 1.2, because these digits refer to different underlying units, namely, hundredths and tenths. Thinking of 1.2 in terms of money, as 1 dollar and 2 dimes, gives students another way to see why adding the 2 in 1.2 to the 5 in 3.45 does not make sense, because that would be like saying that 2 dimes plus 5 pennies is 7 pennies. By reasoning this way, students should come to see that they must take care to align like places rather than simply align the rightmost digits. They can also be helped by indicating zero values explicitly by appending zeros so that all the addends have the same number of digits to the right of the decimal point. For example, instead of writing

$$1.2$$
$$+3.45$$

students can write

$$1.20$$
$$+3.45.$$

When regrouping is necessary in addition, the same fundamental property of the decimal system is used whether with whole numbers or decimals, namely, the property that the value of a place is ten times the value of the place to its right, so that 10 in one place can be traded for a 1 in the next place to the left. As with whole-number addition, students can write regrouped digits either above or below the appropriate column of digits, as in figure 3.16b.

As with whole-number subtraction, students can choose to "ungroup all" before beginning to subtract, as shown on the right in figure 3.16b, instead of proceeding column by column ungrouping as necessary. The ungrouping for decimals is done just like that for whole numbers: a 1 in one place can be traded for 10 in the next place to the right.

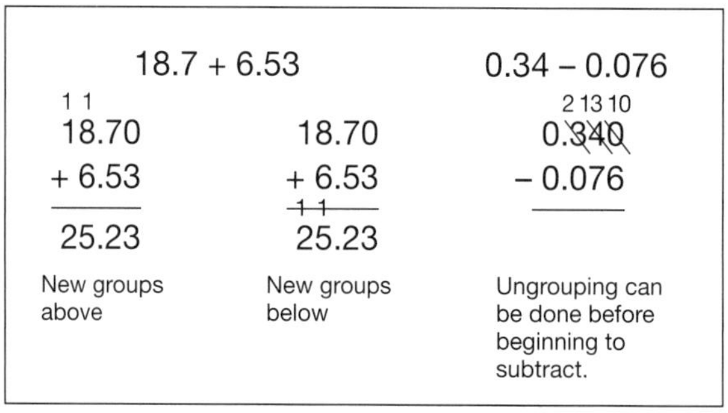

18.7 + 6.53		0.34 − 0.076
1 1 18.70 + 6.53 ——— 25.23	18.70 + 6.53 —1 1— 25.23	2 13 10 0.3̶4̶0̶ − 0.076 ———
New groups above	New groups below	Ungrouping can be done before beginning to subtract.

Fig. 3.16b. Regrouping methods

Students explaining such methods would use place-value language just as they did for whole numbers to show the meanings of the quantities. They might also refer to dimes and pennies in their explanations. For example, a student might explain either of the first two solutions in figure 3.16b as follows: "I added a 0 in the hundredths place for 18 and 7 tenths so I would be adding hundredths to hundredths and not make a mistake aligning my numbers. Then 0 hundredths and 3 hundredths are 3 hundredths, which I wrote in the total place. Seven tenths plus 5 tenths are 12 tenths, which is 10 tenths and 2 tenths, which is 1 and 2 tenths. I write the new 1 in the ones place. Then I add 8 and 6 is 14 and one more is 15. This is 1 ten and 5 ones. I write the 5 ones in the ones place and write the new 1 ten in the tens place. That new ten added to the 10 in 18 makes 2 tens."

Problem Solving with Decimal Addition and Subtraction

1. One juice bottle holds 1.2 liters. Another juice bottle holds 0.35 liters less. How much does the other bottle hold?

   (Answer: 1.2 − 0.35 = 0.85 liters.)

2. One pole is 3.42 meters long. Another pole is 1.8 meters long. How much longer is the longer pole?

   (Answer: 3.42 − 1.8 = 1.62 meters.)

3. A piece of rope 5.88 meters long is attached end to end to another piece of rope. Together, the two joined pieces of rope are 7.2 meters long. How long was the piece of rope that was attached to the first piece?

   (Answer: 7.2 − 5.88 = 1.32 meters.)

4. 0.084 grams of a chemical are mixed with 0.35 grams of another chemical. How much does the mixture weigh?

   (Answer: 0.084 + 0.35 = 0.434 grams.)

5. A pharmacist put 0.73 grams of medicine in a container. After some more medicine was added, there were 2 grams of medicine in the container. How much medicine was added to the container?

   (Answer: 2 − 0.73 = 1.27 grams.)

Connecting Fractions and Decimals

The initial connection between fractions and decimals was discussed previously: Decimals are special fractions (equal parts of a whole) that involve powers of ten (tenths, hundredths, thousandths, etc.). In fourth grade, students begin to learn about the connection between fractions and decimals by expressing fractions as decimals in some restricted, common cases, mainly those that are encountered with money. In fifth, sixth, and later grades, students deepen their understanding of the connection between fractions and decimals through division.

Connecting fractions and decimals in the most common cases

In fourth grade, when students plot numbers on number lines that show different tick marks, they should be prompted to notice that some lengths can be expressed as fractions or as decimals. Fourth graders focus on connecting fractions and decimals in only the simplest and most common instances of fractions less than 1:

$$\frac{1}{2} = 0.5 \qquad \frac{1}{4} = 0.25 \qquad \frac{3}{4} = 0.75$$

$$\frac{1}{10} = 0.1 \quad \frac{2}{10} = 0.2 \quad \frac{3}{10} = 0.3 \quad \frac{4}{10} = 0.4 \quad \frac{5}{10} = 0.5 \quad \frac{6}{10} = 0.6 \quad \frac{7}{10} = 0.7 \quad \frac{8}{10} = 0.8 \quad \frac{9}{10} = 0.9$$

$$\frac{1}{5} = 0.2 \qquad \frac{2}{5} = 0.4 \qquad \frac{3}{5} = 0.6 \qquad \frac{4}{5} = 0.8$$

$$\frac{1}{3} = 0.33\ldots \qquad \frac{2}{3} = 0.66\ldots$$

All these connections can be aided by expressing a fraction of a dollar in terms of cents. For example, the 1/2 and all the tenths and fifths above can be thought of as dimes (1/2 of the 10 dimes in 1 dollar is 5 dimes, so 1/2 = 0.5). The quarters can be thought of as pennies (1 dollar divided into 4 equal parts is 25 cents, or one quarter = 0.25). Even thirds can be found by thinking of dividing one dollar into three equal shares: 1/3 of a dollar is the amount of money each person gets if $1 is divided equally among 3 people. To divide $1 equally among 3 people, each person can first get 3 dimes (0.3). Then the remaining 10 cents can be divided by giving each person 3 cents. Now each person has 33 cents, or $0.33, but one penny still remains that we cannot split because we do not have fractions of a cent. For this reason, we must indicate that the decimal representation for 1/3 continues to the right of the hundredths place. If we did have a coin for 1/1000 of a dollar, then 10 of those coins would be worth a cent and each person would get 3 of those coins, leaving one of those coins remaining. Continuing with this reasoning would show that the decimal representation of 1/3 is 0.33333…, where the 3s continue without end. Understanding these equivalences between simple fractions and decimals can increase students' flexibility in problem solving and enhance their understanding of both fractions and decimals.

Writing hundredths and thousandths as decimals, and saying decimals

The reasoning that underlies the sense of saying decimals in the conventional way involves equivalent fractions and thus can be done only informally before students have learned how to make equivalent fractions. This reasoning also explains why we can write hundredths, thousandths, ten-thousandths, and so on, as decimals.

Consider the example 0.23. We say "twenty-three hundredths" for 0.23, whereas by the way 0.23 was defined, it is 2 tenths and 3 hundredths. Notice that the reason these two different representations should stand for the same number will not be immediately obvious to students. However, if students view 2 tenths as 20 hundredths, then "2 tenths and 3 hundredths" is equal to "20 hundredths and 3 hundredths," which is equal to "23 hundredths." In terms of money, "2 tenths and 3 hundredths" can be thought of as "2 dimes and 3 pennies." When the 2 dimes are traded for 20 pennies, the total amount becomes "23 pennies." Expressed with conventional mathematical symbols, "twenty-three hundredths" means 23/100, whereas 0.23 means "2 tenths and 3 hundredths," or 2/10 + 3/100. Since

$$\frac{2}{10} = \frac{2 \times 10}{10 \times 10} = \frac{20}{100},$$

it follows that

$$0.23 = \frac{2}{10} + \frac{3}{100} = \frac{20}{100} + \frac{3}{100} = \frac{23}{100}.$$

The same reasoning shows that in any (finite) decimal, each digit can be expressed in terms of the value of the rightmost digit in the decimal, and therefore the entire decimal can be expressed in terms of the value of the rightmost nonzero digit. For example, the rightmost nonzero digit in 0.0037 is in the ten-thousandths place, and 0.0037 is 30 ten-thousandths and 7 ten-thousandths, which is 37 ten-thousandths. Similarly, 1.234 is 1234 thousandths.

Reversing the foregoing reasoning shows that hundredths, thousandths, ten-thousandths, and so on, can be expressed as decimals. For example,

$$\frac{62}{100} = \frac{60}{100} + \frac{2}{100} = \frac{6}{10} + \frac{2}{100} = 0.62,$$

$$\frac{234}{1000} = \frac{200}{1000} + \frac{30}{1000} + \frac{4}{1000} = \frac{2}{10} + \frac{3}{100} + \frac{4}{1000} = 0.234.$$

Since *percent* stands for "hundredths," students can connect percents with fractions and decimals once they know how to connect hundredths with decimals.

Decimal representations of fractions

In fifth or sixth grade, once students understand the connection between fractions and division (see the previous discussion on fractions and division), they can begin to express fractions as decimals by dividing. The equivalences they found by thinking of money can be found by long division into decimal places. Decimal representations for less-simple fractions can then be found using such long division. For example, to determine the decimal representation of 2/7, students calculate 2 ÷ 7 to obtain 0.285714.... Students should notice that the block of digits, 285714, repeats without end. In later grades, students use the repetitive nature of the division algorithm to explain why the decimal representation of a fraction must always either repeat or terminate.

The continuing connection between fractions and decimals

We close this section on fractions and decimals by emphasizing again points made at several places: Fractions and decimals have different notations that dictate details of operations with each of them. But the big ideas about these operations apply both to fractions and to decimals. To add, subtract, and compare, the solver must add, subtract, or compare like units. Sometimes preliminary work must be done to get like units (such as finding equivalent fractions or ungrouping when subtracting mixed numbers or decimals).

4 Two- and Three- Dimensional Shapes, and Area and Volume

Why study the familiar three-dimensional geometrical shapes, namely, prisms, pyramids, cylinders, cones, and spheres? And why study the area of two-dimensional shapes and the surface area and volume of three-dimensional shapes?

In addition to length, area (including surface area) and volume are the geometric ways to describe the size of objects. Area tells us how much material is required to cover a two-dimensional shape or to cover the outer surfaces of a three-dimensional shape. Volume tells us how much material is required to fill a three-dimensional shape.

One reason to study the familiar three-dimensional geometric shapes is that these shapes are relatively simple and we can view many of the physical objects around us as composed of approximate versions of them. The trunks of many trees are approximately in the shape of a cylinder (or perhaps more accurately, a portion of a cone), most rooms are roughly the shape of a prism whose bases are the floor and ceiling, a pile of gravel might be cone-shaped, and a bottle might be roughly a combination of a cylinder and a cone. By studying the surface area and volume of the basic shapes, students develop important tools for describing the size of objects in the world around us.

Essential to understanding volume and surface area of three-dimensional shapes is viewing shapes as composed of other shapes. We usually calculate surface areas and develop formulas for surface areas by viewing the outer surface of a shape as consisting of several pieces joined together. We often calculate volumes and develop formulas for volumes by viewing a shape as decomposed into pieces or layers. Thus the study of area and volume gives students the opportunity to engage in one of the most common and powerful ways of reasoning in mathematics: that of taking apart, analyzing piece by piece, and putting the analysis together to draw a conclusion. Of prime importance in the study of area and volume is the *reasoning* that leads to the common area and volume formulas. This reasoning connects the geometry of the shape with the algebra of the area or volume formula.

The next section discusses the main ideas leading up to, and in, the fifth-grade focus on area of shapes.

Progression of ideas about, and related to, area of flat two-dimensional shapes

Grade 1	Compose and decompose shapes (e.g., putting two triangles together to make a rhombus; decomposing a hexagon into 6 triangles, 3 rhombuses, or 2 trapezoids; tiling rectangles with squares).
Grade 3	Initially, find the number of objects in a rectangular array by counting one by one. Then recognize the structure of arrays as groups of rows or groups of columns, and use multiplication to find the number of items in a rectangular array. Include the case of rectangles decomposed into arrays of touching squares.
	Investigate, describe, and reason about decomposing, combining, and transforming polygons to make other polygons (include attending to angles and side lengths, and include making composite shapes that are treated as a unit and repeated). In the case of rectangles decomposed as arrays of touching squares, rotate these and view them as made by combining smaller arrays to show to properties of multiplication (e.g., the commutative property, the distributive property).
Grade 4	Understand that the area of a shape (in square units) is the number of unit squares required to cover the shape without gaps or overlaps.
	Fill simple shapes with unit squares, or use graph paper to determine areas, cutting squares in half if necessary so that no gaps or overlaps occur. Realize that shapes that look different can have the same area.
	Distinguish area from perimeter: two shapes can have the same area but different perimeter; two shapes can have the same perimeter but different area. Use graph paper or square tiles and rods or string to see why.
	Understand that areas of rectangles can be found by multiplying two adjacent side lengths because of the way rectangles can be decomposed into arrays of touching squares (restrict to the case of whole-number side length).
	Understand that different units of area (e.g., square yards or square feet, square meters or square centimeters) can be used to describe the area of a given shape. When a larger unit of area is used, the area is a smaller number of those units.

Grade 4	Understand that areas of shapes can be found by decomposing the shapes into (non-overlapping) pieces, finding the area of each piece, and adding. Restrict mainly to shapes that can be decomposed into rectangular pieces. Decomposing rectangles (or rectangular arrays) according to the place value of the side lengths is essential to explaining the multiplication algorithm.
Grade 5	Combine shapes to find an area (e.g., two congruent right triangles combine to make a rectangle, so we see that the area of the triangle is half the area of the rectangle). Decompose shapes, and move the pieces to find an area. Find an area by viewing a shape as a "difference" of two shapes (taking away area).
	Understand that area formulas for triangles and parallelograms can be found and explained by decomposing and composing to make rectangles. Any side can be chosen to be the base for a triangle or parallelogram, and the area formulas are still true. Different reasoning is often required for establishing validity of the area formula, depending on which side is chosen as base. Apply area formulas to solve problems.
	Find areas of complex shapes made from rectangles, triangles, and parallelograms (note that trapezoids and regular polygons can be viewed as such complex shapes).
Grade 6	Extend the area formula for rectangles to the case of fractional or decimal side lengths.
	Know that area formulas are valid even when side lengths are fractions or decimals. Apply area formulas for rectangles, triangles, and parallelograms in these cases.
Grade 7	See that the area formula for circles is plausible by decomposing circles into wedges (sectors) and rearranging the wedges to form a shape that approximates a parallelogram (or rectangle).
Grade 8	Explain why the Pythagorean theorem is true by decomposing a suitable square in different ways and equating the sum of the areas of the pieces.

Area of Polygons

To make sense of area calculations and area formulas, students must first understand what area is. Area is part of the focus of grade 4.

Measures of area, and units of area

What is area? In fourth grade (or before) students should see a need for the concept of area. The need for area is prompted by the desire to compare the sizes of shapes and to describe the size of a shape succinctly to others. To pique students' interest about area, students can be given two rectangles (which students might view as maps of plots of land), the first of which is wider but shorter than the second, so that which (if either) of the two rectangular plots is bigger is not immediately obvious (for example, see the rectangles in fig. 4.1a). How does one determine which is bigger? How can one describe the size of a rectangle? These questions lead naturally into the study of area.

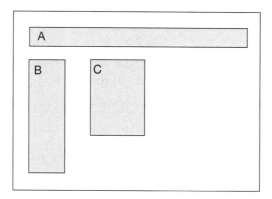

Fig. 4.1a. Which quilt piece covers the most space?

One challenge in learning about area is to understand what area measures. The area of a flat shape is a measure of the amount of space inside the shape; it tells us how much material is needed to cover the shape. As with length, we need standard units of area to be able to communicate clearly. Squares make especially nice units of area because they fit together snugly to make neat rectangular arrays. For this reason, we use squares for our standard units of area. A square centimeter, 1 cm^2, which is the area of a 1-centimeter-by-1-centimeter square, is a natural first unit of area to use. Alternatively, a square inch, 1 in^2, could be used initially. The area of a shape, in square units, is the number of 1-unit-by-1-unit squares ("unit squares") needed to cover the shape without gaps or overlaps.

The students in Ms. C's class discovered the usefulness of a unit square for comparing areas when they were asked which of three quilt pieces, like those shown in figure 4.1, covers the most space (Lehrer et al. 1998). To make the rectangles in figure 4.1a, use the following dimensions: A is 1 by 12, B is 2 by 6, and C is 3 by 4 (but do not give students these dimensions).

One student showed that pieces A and C cover the same amount of space by folding C into four equal horizontal parts. Another student folded C into three equal vertical parts to reach the same conclusion (see fig. 4.1b). When both sets of folds were made on C, the students were able to use the resulting squares as a common unit to show that all three quilt pieces cover the same amount of space.

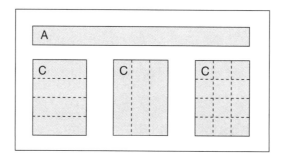

Fig.4.1b. Different ways to compare quilt pieces A and C

Initial area work should involve only whole numbers of units, but students should eventually work with shapes that need to be cut apart and rearranged to make a whole number of unit squares. Initial examples can include triangles of area 1 cm^2, such as a right triangle with 1 cm and 2 cm legs.

By drawing a variety of shapes on graph paper or by making shapes out of tiles (perhaps in a context, such as designing a floor plan for a guinea pig cage), students should come to understand that many different shapes have the same area.

Area versus perimeter

One challenge for students is to understand the distinction between length and area. In fourth grade, students should have the opportunity to distinguish between the area and the perimeter of a shape and to realize that neither one determines the other.

For example, by using a fixed number of rods of a fixed length to make the outline of various different shapes, or by considering or making drawings on graph paper, students could see that two shapes can have the same perimeter but different areas. Because the lengths of two adjacent sides of a rectangle add to half the perimeter of the rectangle, to find rectangles of a given, fixed perimeter, say, 12 feet, find lengths that add to 6 feet. So a 5-foot-by-1-foot rectangle, a 4-foot-by-2-foot rectangle, and a 3-foot-by-3-foot rectangle (and even a 4½-foot-by-1½-foot rectangle) all have the same perimeter, 12 feet, but have different areas.

Students could also arrange square tiles in different configurations or use drawings on graph paper to show that two shapes can have the same area but different perimeter. Given a fixed (whole) number of square-inch tiles, say, twenty-four tiles, finding all the ("filled in") rectangles that can be made with exactly that many tiles is the same as finding the pairs of factors for 24:

$$24 = 1 \times 24, \qquad 24 = 2 \times 12, \qquad 24 = 3 \times 8, \qquad 24 = 4 \times 6.$$

Note that if students take orientation into account, they may think of a pair of factors as giving rise to two rectangles, such as a 3-by-8 rectangle and an 8-by-3 rectangle. These two rectangles are congruent because one can be rotated to match the other, so in an abstract setting, a factor pair produces a single rectangle. But in many practical situations, such as when a rectangular patio is attached to the side of a house, the different orientations can be distinct.

Students who have already studied areas of rectangles might also solve the next Puppy Run and Farmer's Gardens problems.

Puppy Run

You want to make a run for your new puppy. You have 36 feet of fencing. The floor of the puppy run will be in the shape of a rectangle, and the fence will go all the way around the rectangle.

1. Find the lengths of the sides of at least 3 different puppy runs that you could make using all 36 feet of fencing. (Answers vary: Adjacent sides add to 18 feet.)

2. Find the areas of the floors of your puppy runs in part 1. Are all the areas the same? (Answer: The areas are different.)

3. What do you think is the largest area you can make with this amount of fencing? Explain your answer. (Answer: the largest area that can be made occurs when the pen is a 9-foot-by-9-foot square of area 81 square feet. Some students may notice that the more "squarelike" the rectangle is, the greater the area, whereas the greater the difference between lengths of adjacent sides, the smaller the area.)

Areas of rectangles

Farmer's Gardens

A farmer has three gardens. Each garden has a perimeter of 36 feet. The first garden has an area of 81 square feet. The second garden has an area of 72 square feet. The third garden has an area of 45 square feet. What might the dimensions of each garden be? (Answer: If the gardens are rectangular, then two adjacent sides must add to 18 feet (half of 36), so students can look for numbers that add to 18. A 9-foot-by-9-foot garden has area 81 square feet. A 6-foot-by-12-foot-garden has area 72 square feet. A 15-foot-by-3-foot garden has area 45 square feet.

The multiplication formula for areas of rectangles

Why can we multiply the length and width of a rectangle to find its area? A rectangle whose length and width are whole numbers of units can be decomposed into an array of unit squares. By viewing these arrays as groups of rows or groups of columns, as in figure 4.2, students should come to see that they can use multiplication, rather than count one by one, to determine the total number of unit squares covering the rectangle in an efficient way. Thus students should see that the length-times-width formula for areas of rectangles makes sense by viewing rectangles whose sides are whole numbers of units as arrays of unit squares that can be decomposed into equal groups by the rows or the columns of the array. For consistency with other area formulas (for triangles and parallelograms), instead of referring to the side lengths of a rectangle as "length" and "width," we can instead use "base" and "height."

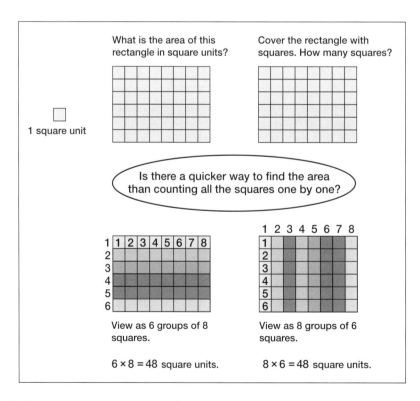

Fig. 4.2. Decomposing a rectangle into groups of squares to see why we multiply

For some students, a challenge in learning the area formula for rectangles is to see that rectangles of whole-number side length can be decomposed into neat arrays of unit squares and that these arrays can be decomposed into equal groups. Such students may need to work with actual squares or make drawings of rows and columns on square grid paper. They need to build rectangles and create mental images of the interior space of rectangles as composed of arrays of squares. Being able to view rectangles as decomposed into groups of squares is essential to understanding the area formula for rectangle.

Rectangle Area Problems

1. A rectangular patio is 8 feet wide and has area 120 square feet. How long is the patio?

   (Answer: 15 feet)

2. A rectangular garden is 25 meters wide and is surrounded by 120 meters of fencing. What is the area of the garden?

   (Answer: The length of the garden is 35 meters because the length plus width is half of the perimeter. So the area is 25 × 35, or 875, square meters.)

3. A rectangle is 40 millimeters wide and 7 centimeters long. What is the area of the rectangle? Why can we not multiply 7 × 40 to find the area?

   (Answer: 28 square centimeters, or 2800 square millimeters. We have to use the same units for the length and the width when we apply the area formula.)

Finding areas of regions composed of several rectangles

In preparation for finding areas of triangles and parallelograms in grade 5 by decomposing and combining shapes, fourth-grade students should become flexible in decomposing shapes into rectangular pieces to find the area. L-shaped regions, such as the one at the top of figure 4.3, are good starting points because students may find several different ways to determine the area, such as the four methods shown in the figure. Although method 4 does not work for all L-shaped regions, it does work in this instance, and it previews a method for determining areas of triangles. Asking students to associate strategies with the corresponding numerical expressions for the area (shown below each strategy in fig. 4.3) forges a connection with algebra.

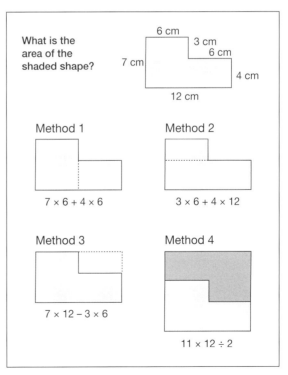

Fig. 4.3. Finding the area of an L-shaped region in several ways

L-shaped Polygons of Area 84

The area of a mystery "L shaped" polygon is 84 square units. What are the lengths of the sides of this mystery polygon? Can we tell for sure, or is more than one L-shaped polygon of area 84 square units possible?

(Answer: Many different L-shaped polygons have area 84 square units.)

Changing the Shape but Keeping the Area the Same

This is a good, challenging multistep problem about area.

The shaded shape is a diagram of a lot. If we want to make the lot into the rectangle *ABCD* of the same area, how long should *CD* be?

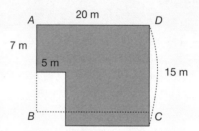

(Answer: 13 meters because the area of the shape is 260 square meters and 260 ÷ 20 = 13)

Other units of area

When students first start studying area in fourth grade (or before), they will use square inches or square centimeters as units. Wanting to describe the area of a room or a field presents the need for other units of area. Square meters and square feet are natural choices of units for describing areas of rooms, fields, and the like. Square kilometers and square miles are natural choices for describing areas of cities, states, and countries.

Students should understand that the area of a region can be given in square meters or in square centimeters but that the number of square meters will be less than the number of square centimeters (and similarly for square feet and square inches). More specifically, students should understand why 100×100 square centimeters are in a square meter and why 12×12 square inches are in a square foot.

When considering area in real-world situations, problems involving estimation are especially appropriate.

Area of a Classroom in Square Feet and Square Yards

1. Tell students: A fourth- (or fifth-) grade class at another school says that their classroom has area approximately 70 square yards. Is our classroom larger, smaller, or about the same? First, make an estimate of the area of our classroom. Then make a plan to determine the area of our classroom.

2. Discuss students' estimates and plans, then ask them to carry out one (or several) of the plans. After students have carried out the plans, have a class discussion in which students compare their answers with their estimates and with the estimate of the other fourth- (or fifth-) grade class.

3. Ask students: What if the other fourth- (or fifth-) grade class reported the area of their classroom in square feet instead of as 70 square yards. Would the number of square feet be greater than or fewer than 70? How do you know?

4. Ask students: Is there a way we can find out the area of the other classroom in square feet, given that it is 70 square yards? (Students should determine that since a 1-yard-by-1-yard square is 3-feet-by-3-feet, 1 square yard is 9 square feet, so 70 square yards is 70 × 9, or 630, square feet.)

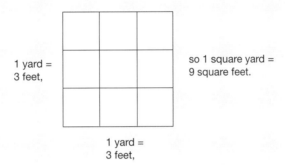

1 yard = 3 feet,   so 1 square yard = 9 square feet.

1 yard = 3 feet,

5. As an optional follow-up, take students on a "field trip" through the school building. Have students estimate various areas. Take measurements so that the areas can be determined at a later time. Back in the classroom, have students determine the areas using the measurements, then compare their answers with their estimates.

Areas of parallelograms, triangles, and other polygons

Since students study many polygons other than combinations of rectangles, a natural extension is to ask about finding areas of familiar polygons. Finding areas of many of these familiar polygons is a focus in grade 5. A central idea is that we can often find the area of a polygon by relating it to another polygon whose area we already know how to find. In particular, parallelograms and triangles can be related to rectangles. Triangles can also be related to parallelograms.

Areas of parallelograms

To help students reason about areas of parallelograms and develop and understand an area formula for parallelograms, students could be given parallelograms on centimeter graph paper and asked to relate them to rectangles to find the area. Students might come up with several different methods, including those indicated in figure 4.4. In each of these cases, the area of the parallelogram is the same as the area of the related rectangle because pieces of the parallelogram have just been rearranged, but no area has been taken away or added. By being asked to compare various lengths on the parallelogram and the rectangle, students should see that the parallelogram has the same base and height as the rectangle. Because the area of the rectangle is base × height and the area of the parallelogram is the same as that of the rectangle, students should see that the area of the parallelogram is also base × height. To understand this reasoning about area and to examine the methods of figure 4.4, students (and teachers!) will benefit from working with multiple cutout copies of a parallelogram. The original parallelogram should be kept intact while the other copies are cut apart and rearranged to make rectangles that have the same base and height as the original parallelogram.

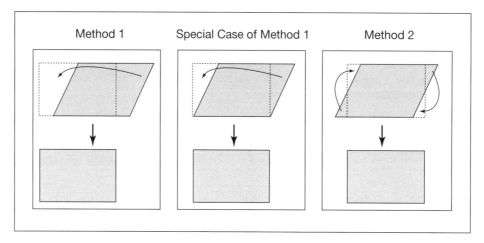

Fig. 4.4. Relating a parallelogram to a rectangle so as to relate the areas

Students should understand that the formula for the area of a parallelogram, base × height, is valid even if the base is chosen so that the parallelogram is "very oblique," as in figure 4.5. Although the methods of figure 4.4 no longer work directly on the very oblique parallelogram in figure 4.5, the parallelogram can be subdivided so that previous methods can be used.

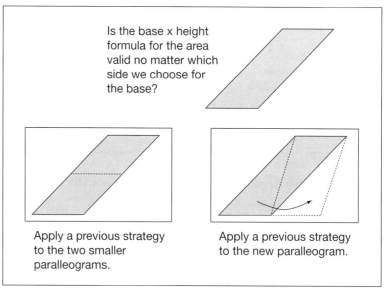

Fig. 4.5. The area formula for parallelograms is valid no matter what base is chosen.

Areas of triangles

To help students reason about areas of triangles and develop and understand an area formula for triangles, students could be given triangles on graph paper and asked to relate the triangles to shapes whose area they already know how to determine. A right triangle is the easiest type of triangle to work with. Students might develop several methods for relating their right triangle to a rectangle, including the two methods shown in figure 4.6. Using the first method, students should see that the area of the triangle is half the area of the associated rectangle. Using the second method, students should see that the area of the triangle is the same as that of the associated rectangle that has half the base. Either way, once they find the area of the associated rectangle, they can find the area of the original triangle. Also, this reasoning establishes that the area of the triangle is (base × height) ÷ 2. Using the first method, the most natural formulation of the formula is (base × height) ÷ 2, whereas using the second method, the most natural formulation is (base ÷ 2) × height. To understand this reasoning about area and to examine the methods of figure 4.6, students (and teachers!) will benefit from working with multiple cutout copies of a right triangle. The original triangle should be kept intact while the other copies are either joined or cut apart and rearranged.

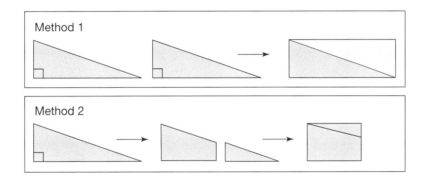

Fig. 4.6. Relating a right triangle to a rectangle to determine the area

Next, students might work with such triangles as the one in figure 4.7, and examine several methods for relating the triangle either to a rectangle or to a parallelogram (if areas of parallelograms have already been studied). Again, students can find and examine methods by cutting apart paper triangles. Using method 1, students should see that the area of the triangle is half the area of the associated rectangle, so that they can find the area of the triangle once they find the area of the rectangle. Using this reasoning, students should be able to explain why the formula (base × height) ÷ 2 for areas of triangles is valid even in this instance.

Students should understand that the formula (base × height ÷ 2) for areas of triangles is valid no matter what side of the triangle is chosen as the base, including instances in which the base is chosen so that the triangle is "very oblique," as in figure 4.8.

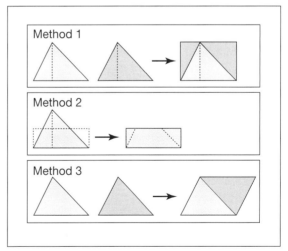

Fig. 4.7. Relating a triangle to a rectangle or parallelogram to find the area

Students might examine several methods for relating the oblique triangle to other shapes whose area they can determine, such as a parallelogram, the "difference" of two right triangles, or a rectangle.

Because many students forget to divide by 2 when finding areas of triangles, a useful tactic is to highlight the relationship between triangles and parallelograms: two copies of a triangle joined along a side of the same length produce a parallelogram, as shown in method 1 of figure 4.6 (where the parallelogram is a rectangle), method 3 of figure 4.7, and method 1 of figure 4.8.

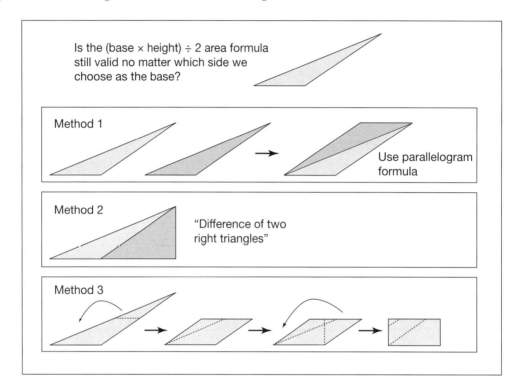

Fig. 4.8. The triangle area formula is valid no matter what base is chosen.

Areas of complex shapes

Once students are able to use the area formulas for rectangles, parallelograms, and triangles, they can apply these formulas to find areas of complex shapes that are combinations of rectangles, parallelograms, and triangles.

In addition to applying the area formulas they have learned, students can also apply the reasoning they used in explaining the formulas. For example, to find the area of the shaded triangle shown at the top right in "Area Problem Solving," students can either view the triangle as having base 6 cm and height 5 cm and apply the triangle area formula, or they can view the shaded triangle as a right triangle with base 12 cm and height 5 cm from which is removed a right triangle of base 6 cm and height 5 cm.

Students might be asked to develop and understand the area formula for trapezoids by decomposing trapezoids into triangles or by relating trapezoids to parallelograms.

Students can find areas of pentagons, hexagons, and other polygons (including regular polygons whose sides all have the same length) by viewing them as complex shapes that can be decomposed into triangles, for example. Enough information about various lengths needs to be given so that students can apply suitable area formulas.

Area Problem Solving

Determine the areas of the shaded shapes.

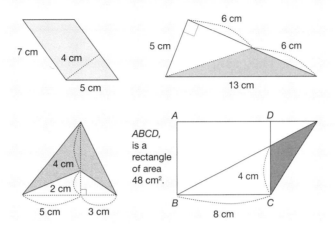

(Answers: top left: 28 cm² because the parallelogram has base 7 cm and height 4 cm; top right: 15 cm² because the triangle has base 6 cm and height 5 cm, or view as the "difference" of two right triangles; bottom left: 16 cm², view as two joined triangles each with base 4 cm or as the "difference" of two triangles each with base 8 cm; bottom right: 8 cm², view as a triangle with base 8 cm and height 6 cm "minus" a right triangle with base 8 cm and height 4 cm.)

Extending the area formulas to decimal and fraction side lengths

When students study multiplication of decimals and fractions in sixth grade, they learn that the formulas for areas of rectangles, triangles, and parallelograms still apply to shapes with decimal and fraction side lengths. Problems involving estimation are especially appropriate with these topics.

Solid Shapes, and Their Volume and Surface Area

Three-dimensional shapes have an outer surface as well as an interior, and the study of solid shapes involves coordinating their two- and three-dimensional aspects. In third grade, students analyze two-dimensional polygons by examining the number and nature of their sides and angles. Similarly, in fifth grade students examine the number and nature of the faces, edges, and vertices of three-dimensional polyhedra. And just as perimeter and area are measurable attributes of two-dimensional shapes that students study in third, fourth, and fifth grades, surface area and volume are measurable attributes of three-dimensional shapes that students focus on in sixth and seventh grades.

Progression of ideas about solid shapes and their volume and surface area

Pre-K, K, Grade 1	Find solid shapes in the environment, describe solid shapes, identify and name them, combine solid shapes to construct more complex shapes, compose and decompose solid shapes.
Grade 5	Describe solid shapes, attending to faces, edges, and vertices. Build shapes with blocks. Make and use drawings of solid shapes. Understand that solid shapes have an outer surface as well as an interior.
	Understand that the volume of a solid shape (in cubic units) is the number of unit cubes required to make (or fill) the shape without gaps (or overlaps).
	Begin to explore volume by predicting the number of cubes that will be needed to make a shape.
	Understand that solid shapes that look different can have the same volume. See why by building different shapes with a fixed number of cubes.
	Initially, find volumes of rectangular prisms by counting cubes one by one. Then recognize the structure of three-dimensional arrays as layers, each of which also has an array structure, and use multiplication to find volume of rectangular prisms.
	Understand that rectangular prisms can be decomposed into three-dimensional arrays of cubes made of layers. The volume of rectangular prisms can be found by multiplying lengths (restrict to whole-number lengths).
	Understand that different units of volume (e.g., cubic inches or cubic feet, cubic meters or cubic centimeters) can be used to describe the volume of a given solid shape. When a larger unit of volume is used, the volume is a smaller number of those units.
	Understand that the surface area of a solid shape is the total area of the outer surface of the shape.
Grade 5	Understand that volume is distinct from surface area. Know the distinction between the units of measure for surface area and volume (square units versus cubic units). Use patterns (nets) and cubes to help distinguish volume from surface area.
	Use patterns (nets) to understand surface area. Determine surface area of solid shapes, focusing on prisms.
Grade 6	The volume formula for rectangular prisms is valid even when the side lengths are decimals or fractions.
	Given two out of three of the following pieces of information about a rectangle, triangle, or parallelogram, solve for the unknown piece of information: the base, the height, the area. Given three out of the following four pieces of information about a rectangular prism, solve for the unknown piece of information: the length, the width, the height, the volume.

Grade 7	Decompose (physically and mentally) prisms (triangular, rectangular, etc.) and cylinders by slicing them to develop and understand formulas for their volumes (area of base times the height). Apply formulas to solve problems.
	Decompose (physically and mentally) surfaces of prisms and cylinders to develop, justify, and understand formulas for their surface areas. Solve problems involving surface area.
Grade 8 or later	Understand why the volume formula for pyramids and cones (one-third of the base times the height) is plausible, and use the formula to solve problems.
	Work with patterns for, and the surface area of, pyramids and cones; for example, given that a cone or pyramid is to have specified dimensions, determine the shape and dimensions of a pattern for the cone or pyramid.

Analyzing solid shapes

Fifth-grade students examine the attributes and structure of solid shapes in various ways, including identifying the faces, edges, and vertices of polyhedra. For example, students could be asked to compare and contrast rectangular prisms and cubes by attending to the number of faces, edges, and vertices, as well as to the nature of the faces and to which faces are identical (congruent). Students could also be asked which faces in a rectangular prism are parallel to a given face, which faces are perpendicular to the face, which edges are parallel to a given edge, and which edges are perpendicular to the edge. Such an analysis of rectangular prisms could then be followed by a discussion on the way we represent points in space by a triple of numbers, such as the point (3, 2, 4), as shown in figure 5.1.

Students might also compare and contrast prisms, cylinders, pyramids, and cones. Fifth-grade students also explore two-dimensional representations of three-dimensional objects by making nets (two-dimensional patterns that can be cut out and folded without overlaps to form the shape), by forming solid shapes from nets, and by predicting what shape a net will make. In particular, fifth graders make patterns for rectangular prisms of specified dimensions. Given a pattern for a rectangular prism, students could predict the number of blocks needed to fill the prism and then check whether their prediction was correct, as in the next activity, "How Many Cubes Do the Boxes Hold?"

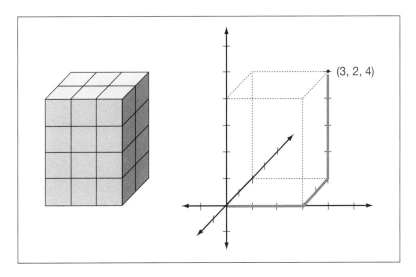

Fig. 5.1. A prism, and representing points in space with coordinates

How Many Cubes Do the Boxes Hold?

Materials: A set of at least 32 cubes for each group of students; graph paper—the spacing between the grid lines must match the edge length of the cubes; tape. Each student should make or be provided with patterns for three open-top boxes made from graph paper, as shown (variation: use only the first two patterns).

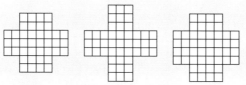

1. Have students do the following for each box, in turn:

    a. Before students fold up the flaps to make the box, ask students to visualize the box and to predict how many cubes the box will hold.

    b. Have students make the box and check their prediction. (Answers: left box: 24 cubes, middle box: 27 cubes, right box: 32 cubes.)

2. Have students share their findings. Note that some students might predict (incorrectly) that the number of cubes a box can hold is the number of squares in the pattern. (See the discussion below on volume versus surface area.)

Fifth-grade students then are better prepared to explore two-dimensional representations of three-dimensional objects by making drawings. For example, students might be asked to make drawings to show the appearance of a structure made of blocks from different viewpoints. Students might also build a block structure on the basis of drawings of the appearance of the structure from the top, the front, and the side.

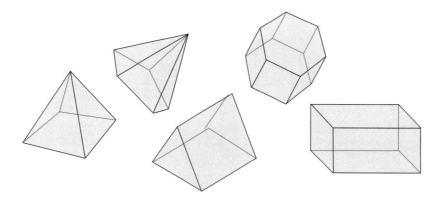

Measures of volume, and units of volume

What is volume? In fifth grade (or before), students should see a need for the concept of volume. The need for volume is prompted by the desire to describe how much material is needed to fill, or how much space is inside, a three-dimensional shape or to compare the sizes of three-dimensional shapes. To pique students' interest in volume, they can be asked which of several shipping boxes can hold more boxes of a fixed size. See also the previous activity, "How Many Cubes Do the Boxes Hold?"

One challenge in learning about volume is to understand the kind of quantity that volume measures and to understand the distinction between surface area and volume. A physical object, such as a box, has a volume, a surface area, and a height, width, and length—all of which are measurable attributes of the same box but which measure different aspects of the box and use different, but related, units.

The volume of a three-dimensional shape is a measure of the amount of material or space enclosed within the shape. As with length and area, we need standard units of volume to communicate clearly.

Cubes make especially nice units of volume because they are uniform and fit together snugly to make neat three-dimensional arrays. For this reason, people customarily use cubes as standard units of volume. Although students might work first with identical cubes of some other size, a cubic centimeter, 1 cm^3, which is the volume of a 1-cm-by-1-cm-by-1-cm cube, is a natural first unit of volume to use. Alternatively, a cubic inch, 1 in^3, could be used initially. The volume of a three-dimensional shape, in cubic units, is the number of 1-unit-by-1-unit-by-1-unit cubes ("unit cubes") required to fill or make the shape without gaps or overlaps.

Although initial volume work will involve only whole numbers of units, students might also be exposed to solid shapes that would need to be cut apart and rearranged to make a whole number of unit cubes.

By making a variety of solid shapes out of a fixed number of cubes, students should come to understand that many different shapes have the same volume (see the activity "Expressions for Volumes of Boxes Made of Twenty-four Cubes" in the section "Other units of volume").

Volumes of rectangular prisms

Is a quicker way available to find the volume of a rectangular prism than counting the number of cubes needed to fill it one by one? Why can we multiply to find the volume of a rectangular prism? These questions are a focus in grade 5. Given rectangular prisms whose length, width, and height are whole numbers of units, we can view the prism as made of a three-dimensional array of unit cubes. By viewing these arrays as consisting of layers (either horizontal or vertical) as in figure 5.2, and noticing that the layers themselves can also be decomposed into equal groups, students should come to realize that they can use multiplication rather than counting one by one to determine the total number of unit cubes required to fill a rectangular prism in an efficient way.

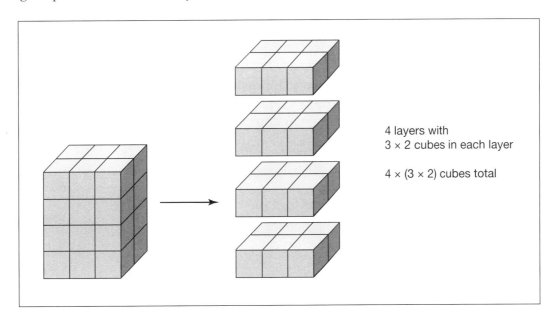

4 layers with
3 × 2 cubes in each layer

4 × (3 × 2) cubes total

Fig. 5.2. Decomposing a rectangular prism to show the grouping structure

To help students begin to understand that they can multiply to find volumes of rectangular prisms, students could do the next activity, "Volumes of Prisms of Varying Height." Students should develop the understanding that the number of cubes in each rectangular prism is the number of cubes in each layer multiplied by the number of layers (which is the height). Each layer can itself be decomposed into equal groups on the basis of the length and width of the layer. This process is just like decomposing a rectangle into rows or columns of squares, except that in this situation, each layer can be viewed as rows or columns of *cubes*. Thus, students should come to understand why they can find the volume of a rectangular prism by multiplying the height, length, and width of the prism. The next activity can help students begin to develop this understanding.

One challenge in learning about volume is to visualize the grouping structure in three-dimensional arrays of cubes. For example, students often do not recognize three-dimensional arrays of cubes as consisting of layers (either vertical or horizontal). When students are given a box shape made of identical cubes, some students may try, incorrectly, to find the total number of cubes in the box by adding the number of cubes visible on each of the four lateral sides of the box, and other students may add the number of cubes visible on all six sides of the box. In some sense, these students are confusing the surface of the box with its volume. Being able to visualize three-dimensional prisms as layers of arrays of cubes is essential to understanding why we can multiply to find volumes of boxes.

Gradually, in fifth grade as well as in higher grades, students can be asked to solve more complex multistep problems concerning volumes of rectangular prisms, such as in the activity titled "Volumes of Prisms of Varying Height." For the second problem, students will need to learn how objects placed under water displace water.

When students study multiplication of decimals and fractions in sixth grade, they should learn that the formula for volumes of rectangular prisms still applies to rectangular prisms with decimal and fractional side lengths.

Other units of volume

The desire to describe the volume of a room or large container, such as a pool or the hold of a truck, prompts the need for units of volume other than the cubic centimeter or cubic inch. Cubic meters, cubic feet, and cubic yards are good units for describing larger volumes. To show a cubic meter, 12 metersticks can be joined with masking tape to form the frame of a 1-meter-by-1-meter-by-1-meter cube.

A natural classroom activity is for students to determine the approximate volume of the classroom in cubic meters (or cubic feet or cubic yards). Students should understand that the volume of a shape or region can be described in cubic meters or in cubic centimeters, but that the number of cubic meters will be less than the number of cubic centimeters (and similarly for cubic feet and cubic inches). More specifically, students should understand why there are $100 \times 100 \times 100 = 1{,}000{,}000$ cubic centimeters in a cubic meter and $12 \times 12 \times 12 = 1728$ cubic inches in a cubic foot. In later grades, students will convert between different units of volume.

Volumes of Prisms of Varying Height

Materials: A set of about 40 cubes for each group of students; graph paper—the spacing between the grid lines must match the edge length of the cubes.

1. Have students outline a rectangle of their choice on the graph paper (not too big).

2. Ask students to build rectangular prisms that have their chosen base and are 1 unit tall, 2 units tall, 3 units tall, and 4 units tall.

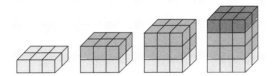

Record the volumes of these prisms in a table:

Area of the base: _____ (square units)

Height (units)	1	2	3	4	20	100
Volume (cubic units)						

3. Ask students how the volume changes as the height changes and what relationships they notice.

4. Using their chosen base, have students predict the volume of a prism that has various heights, such as 20 or 100 units, without continuing the table.

5. Have students repeat with other bases.

Surface area

The study of surface area, and in particular, the surface area of rectangular prisms, is a focus in grade 5. The desire to describe how much material (fabric, paper, cardboard, etc.) is required to cover a solid shape prompts the need for the concept of surface area. The surface area of a solid shape is the total area of the outer surface of the shape. So the surface area of a polyhedron is the combined area of all the faces of the polyhedron. Since a net for a shape forms the outside of the shape, a study of nets is a natural foundation for the study of surface area. Students should understand that to find the surface area of a shape, they should find the area of each piece (e.g., face) of the shape and add those areas to find the total area.

Expressions for Volumes of Boxes Made of Twenty-four Cubes

Each group of students will need 24 cubes of the same size. Call the length of each side 1 unit. Draw students' attention to the layered structure of a rectangular prism box built of cubes: each layer has the same number of cubes in it, and that number is the same as the area of the base. The number of layers is the height of the box. Because of this structure, we can use multiplication to express the total number of cubes in the box.

Task: Find at least six rectangular prisms (boxes) made from 24 cubes. (The 24 cubes should be packed solidly, with no gaps.) Record the information for each prism in the table, which has one example filled in.

Prism no.	Height (units)	Expression for area of base (square units)	Expression for volume (cubic units)	Check that the volume is 24 cubic units
1	4	3×2	$4 \times (3 \times 2)$	$4 \times (3 \times 2) = 4 \times 6 = 24$
2				
3				
4				
5				
6				

In a discussion following the activity, students might consider whether some of the prisms in their list are actually the same, but just in a different orientation. For example, a prism that is 4 layers high and has a 3-by-2 base can be tilted down to form a prism that is only 3 layers high but has a 4-by-2 base. Students could also share methods they used to find new prisms. Some students might have found methods of "halving along one dimension and doubling along another" to find new prisms from existing ones. For example, starting with a prism that has a 3-by-2 base with 4 layers, the top half of the prism (the top 2 layers) can be taken off and moved to the base to make a prism that has a 6-by-2 base with 2 layers. Numerically, this action corresponds to halving the first factor of $4 \times (3 \times 2)$ and then compensating by doubling the second factor to obtain $2 \times (6 \times 2)$.

As an extension, students could be asked to find a way to list all the possible prisms systematically (and then cross off the prisms that are the same but in a different orientation).

As previously discussed, one challenge for students is to distinguish the surface area from the volume of a solid shape. To help students distinguish the surface (or surface area) of a rectangular prism from its volume, students could be given patterns (nets) for boxes, such as the ones in the previously described activity "How Many Cubes Do the Boxes Hold?" (which fold to make open-top boxes) and asked to predict or determine the volume of the boxes (or the number of cubes needed to fill each) either before or after the students make the boxes. These patterns should be chosen so that counting the number of squares on the pattern does not produce the correct volume.

Volume Problems

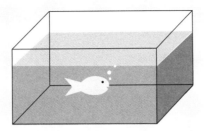

Problem 1: A fish tank in the shape of a rectangular prism is 20 cm wide, 40 cm long, and 20 cm tall. At first, the fish tank is filled to the top with water. When 2400 cm^3 of water is poured out, then how high is the water level in the tank?

[Answer: 17 cm. Students might reason that the water that is poured out would take up the top 3 cm of the tank, since the area of the base is 800 cm^2.]

Problem 2: A fish tank in the shape of a rectangular prism is 20 cm wide and 28 cm long. The fish tank contained some water and a stone that was completely under water. When the stone was taken out, the water level dropped by 2 cm. What is the volume of the stone?

[Answer: 1120 cm^3]

Problem 3: An empty tank that is in the shape of a rectangular prism that is 25 cm by 30 cm by 20 cm will be filled with water from a hose. (a) How many liters of water will be needed to fill the tank? [Students will need to know that 1 liter of liquid fills a cube that is 10 cm by 10 cm by 10 cm and therefore has volume 1000 cm^3.] (b) If 5 liters of water flow out of the hose and into the tank every minute, how many minutes will be needed to fill the tank?

[Answers: (a) 15 liters; (b) 3 minutes]

Activity: What Is the Volume of Our Classroom?

Materials: Tape measures or metersticks/yard sticks. Have a cube of volume 1 cubic meter (or 1 cubic yard, or 1 cubic foot, depending on which unit the students will use) available for students to see.

1. Before they do any measuring, ask students to estimate the volume of the classroom and write down their estimate.

2. Ask students to make a plan for determining the approximate volume of the classroom. Their plans should include taking measurements. Discuss students' plans. Have students carry out their plans, then compare their answers with their initial estimates.

To help students understand that rectangular prisms of the same volume can have different surface area, students might do the next activity, "Same Volume, Different Surface Area.

Same Volume, Different Surface Area

Materials: 24 cubes for each group of students

1. Ask students to determine the surface area (in square units) of various different rectangular prisms of volume 24 cubic units. (See the activity "Expressions for Volumes of Boxes Made of Twenty-four Cubes.") The problem can be posed in terms of finding how much cardboard would be needed to cover the outside of the various boxes containing 24 cubes.

2. Ask students to determine which rectangular prism has the least surface area. As a context, a company that makes boxes holding 24 cubes might want to use the least amount of cardboard so as to make the least expensive box.

3. Lead a discussion on surface area versus volume.

Make a Net to Determine Surface Area

Materials: Centimeter graph paper, scissors, tape

Essential question: How can we find the surface area of a rectangular prism?

1. Ask students to make nets (patterns) for a rectangular prism that is 4 cm by 5 cm by 6 cm.

2. Have students cut out their nets and form their prisms.

3. Ask students to determine the surface area of their prisms.

4. Ask students to predict the surface area of a prism that is 10 cm by 15 cm by 20 cm without making a pattern.

5. Lead a discussion about finding the surface area of rectangular prisms. Some students might begin to notice that for each pair of numbers among the length, width, and height are two faces that have that pair of dimensions. For example, a 4-by-5-by-6 prism has two 4-by-5 faces, two 4-by-6 faces, and two 5-by-6 faces. You might also discuss how surface area is different from volume.

Fifth graders can be given actual objects in the shape of rectangular or triangular prisms or pyramids and asked to determine the surface area by making appropriate measurements and calculations. Fifth graders also use pictures of rectangular or triangular prisms or pyramids to determine their surface areas (provided suitable lengths are supplied in the picture). In general, the surface area of a prism can be found by thinking about the prism as being made of three pieces: the two bases that form the top and bottom (which have the same area) and a rectangle that wraps around the perimeter of the bases to form the lateral part of the prism. The height of this rectangle is the height of the prism. The base (or width) of the rectangle is the perimeter of the base of the prism.

In seventh grade students will determine the surface area of cylinders by viewing the outer surface of a cylinder as consisting of a circular top and bottom and a rectangle that wraps around the circumference of the circles. In eighth grade or later, students will solve problems about patterns for, and the surface area of, pyramids and cones.

References

Donovan, M. Suzanne, and John D. Bransford, eds. *How Students Learn: Mathematics in the Classroom.* Washington, D.C. National Academy Press, 2005.

Fuson, Karen, and Aki Murata. "Integrating NRC Principles and the NCTM Process Standards to Form a Class Learning Path Model That Individualizes within Whole-Class Activities." *National Council of Supervisors of Mathematics Journal of Mathematics Education Leadership* 10, no. 1 (2007): 72–91.

Kilpatrick, Jeremy, Jane Swafford, and Bradford Findell, eds. *Adding It Up: Helping Children Learn Mathematics.* Washington, D.C.: National Academy Press, 2001.

Lehrer, Richard, Cathy Jacobson, Greg Thoyre, Vera Kemeny, Dolores Strom, Jeffrey Horvath, Stephen Gance, and Matthew Koehler. "Developing Understanding of Geometry and Space in the Primary Grades." In *Designing Learning Environments for Developing Understanding of Geometry and Space,* edited by Richard Leher and Daniel Chazan, pp. 169–200. Mahwah, N.J.: Lawrence Erlbaum Associates, 1998.

National Council of Teachers of Mathematics (NCTM). *Principles and Standards for School Mathematics.* Reston, Va.: NCTM, 2000.

———. *Curriculum Focal Points for Prekindergarten through Grade 8 Mathematics.* Reston, Va.: NCTM, 2006.

Schmidt, William H., Curtis C. McKnight, and Senta A. Raizen. *A Splintered Vision: An Investigation of U.S. Science and Mathematics Education.* Dordrecht, Netherlands: Kluwer, 1997.

Stacey, Kaye. "Travelling the Road to Expertise: A Longitudinal Study of Learning." In *Proceedings of the 29th Conference of the International Group for the Psychology of Mathematics Education,* edited by Helen L. Chick and Jill L. Vincent. Melbourne, Australia: PME, 2005.

Stacey, Kaye, Sue Helme, and Vicki Steinle. "Confusions between Decimals, Fractions and Negative Numbers: A Consequence of the Mirror as a Conceptual Metaphor in Three Different Ways." *Psychology of Mathematics Education* 25, no. 4 (2001): 217–24.

Steinle, Vicki, Kaye Stacey, and Diane Chambers. *Teaching and Learning about Decimals.* 2002. CD-ROM. Available from http://extranet.edfac.unimelb.edu.au/DSME/decimals/.

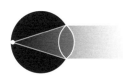
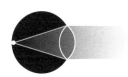